COPS ON A
COLLEGE CAMPUS

by
C. V. Christian

Bloomington, IN  Milton Keynes, UK

authorHOUSE™

AuthorHouse™
1663 Liberty Drive, Suite 200
Bloomington, IN 47403
www.authorhouse.com
Phone: 1-800-839-8640

AuthorHouse™ UK Ltd.
500 Avebury Boulevard
Central Milton Keynes, MK9 2BE
www.authorhouse.co.uk
Phone: 08001974150

First published by AuthorHouse 3/20/2006

ISBN: 1-4259-2398-4 (sc)

Printed in the United States of America
Bloomington, Indiana

This book is printed on acid-free paper.

Dedicated to my loving, patient and understanding wife, Sandra, to my two sons Daniel and Edward who spent many nights and weekends without their father and to the all those heroic law enforcement officers who gave their lives in the performance of their duties.

Introduction

The following pages contain various experiences I have encountered during my 16 year tenure as the Chief Investigator at Georgetown University. Some names have been changed to prevent and to protect certain individuals from embarrassment.

So many people, upon learning of my occupation, would ask "why does a college need a police department?" Numerous people think that all that occurs on a college campus is students going to classes, going to the library, studying, doing term papers, and in general just getting an education. That is true... however some of their education comes with a heavier price than what their tuition was.

It's a pretty rare occasion to have a job that you look forward to going to everyday, but, such was my case at Georgetown University. All the major law enforcement agencies have specialized departments such as Homicide, Burglary, Sex Offense, Check and Fraud, Robbery, etc. My office handled all of these situations which gave me the opportunity to broaden my investigative experiences. Prior to this job I'd had previous experience as a private investigator for various detective agencies throughout the United States in addition to having my own license. I have also studied the martial arts since 1956 and while I was in the U. S. Air Force participated in the first Air Defense Command judo tournament at McChord AFB, Washington. This added knowledge became extremely helpful in various situations that I had encountered both on and off campus.

Our department was composed of a Director, Associate Director, two Assistant Directors, Office Staff, three Shift Supervisors on the main campus and one at the Law Center, four Investigators' and the Identification Card Section. Each shift had their Communications Officers (Dispatchers) and a minimum of eight Patrol Officers. The total amount of Campus Police personnel was between 48 and 55. In addition to this we also had a Student Guard section of twenty students and a Supervisor.

My years at Georgetown University will never be forgotten nor the friends that I had made while I was there. There are numerous times when I think about those years and the people that made it a pleasure to show up for work. I am proud to have made so many friends of students, faculty, staff, and members of other law enforcement agencies. There's not an address book large enough to list them all and even though many years have passed since we have seen each other I still remember everyone.

I would feel remiss if I didn't take this opportunity to express my thanks to the detectives and officers of the Metropolitan Police Department, Arlington County Police Department, Falls Church Police Department, and the Fairfax Police Department. I also owe a debt of gratitude to the Special Agents of the Federal Bureau of Investigation, the Postal Inspectors Office, the Secret Service, the Treasury Department and the Bureau of Alcohol, Tobacco, and Fire Arms. The investigator's for Riggs Bank, and the Bell Atlantic Telephone Company are not forgotten either. And last, but, not the least, in all fairness I also have to express some gratitude to all the thieves, burglars and other miscreants that I had encountered during these years as they kept me employed at Georgetown University, and, without them I wouldn't have been able to write these stories.

Ever since I can remember I had always wanted to be a cop. When I was a little kid back home in Rock Island, Illinois I was a member of the Junior Police Association which was a program sponsored by the Rock Island Police Department. I still have my Junior Police certificate after all these years (which have really been a lot of years).

On 1 September 1974 I retired from the U. S. Air Force with expectations of being a deputy sheriff with the Arlington County Sheriff's Department in Arlington, Virginia. However, upon taking the physical exam it was discovered that I had had two surgical procedures to my left shoulder from recurring dislocations from an injury I had received while undergoing parachute training when I was in the Army at Fort Bragg, North Carolina. In view of this I was disqualified for that position, so, it was back to hunting for a job to support the family as the retired pay of a Technical Sergeant isn't all that much for a family of four.

I lost count of the numerous times I had applied for a law enforcement position and was advised that I was "over qualified". After a week or so I responded to an advertisement in the newspaper for a local security service and two days later I started working for the International Security Corporation as a Road Inspector with the rank of Lieutenant. This was a pretty easy job and the pay wasn't all that bad. My duties mainly consisted of visiting the various security posts we had to ensure the assigned person or persons were performing his/her duties as prescribed by policy and procedure. It was during this period when I met Frank Allen, a fellow part-time employee who worked in the Traffic Department at Georgetown University in Washington, D.C. After a few conversations with him he said he would talk to the Director of the Campus Police about me and let him know that I was interested in a job there. It so happened that there had just been a big shake up in their police department as two of their people (one sergeant and one officer) were arrested for drug dealing among other charges and they were in need of an investigator. A few days later I had received a phone call from the Director, Mr. Charles E. Lamb III, and advised of the necessary procedures for application. I submitted my application and was advised that I would be notified of the results. A couple days after I had submitted my application I was interviewed for the position by Mr. Lamb. After a couple of weeks had gone by following the interview and not hearing anything from the Director I contacted him and he advised me that I had the job, however, there was a certain amount of time that had to pass because the position had to be offered to in-house personnel. Consequently on 1 October 1974 I became the Investigator for that police department. I was processed into the position and obtained my police commission from the Metropolitan Police Department (MPD) which gave me full arrest powers within the District of Columbia.

It so happened that my position was being temporarily filled by another officer who had hopes for the job but didn't get it resulting in a certain amount of animosity from him and an extreme lack of cooperation. Oh well, I figured he'd get over it, but, instead he decided to quit and work someplace else rather than associate with a white person who took his job. Incidentally, he had also filed a complaint of racial discrimination which was dismissed as unfounded.

My first order of business was to do something with the office I was assigned to. The previous person had it painted red, black, and green. I had noticed some paneling in one of the store rooms and asked my boss if I could use it to panel my office to which he agreed. After my tour of duty for the day I stayed to do the paneling of the office and after three days had it looking like an office should look. The record keeping of the case files was atrocious, so, I set up the same filing system as I used while in the Air Force and after two weeks I had the files where you could find what you wanted. Part of my job description was to handle all lost and found items. I took an inventory of the various items that were in the lost and found section. There were numerous bicycles, watches, rings, class rings, books, notebooks, clothing, and various other items. Apparently no one took the time or bother to return any of these items to their proper owner because many of the items were marked with the owners name. I was able to return almost all the books and notebooks to their owners and whatever items were identifiable were returned creating a lot of empty space. The bicycles were offered to the Arlington County Police Department as they sponsored a summer camp for underprivileged youths and the bicycles were repaired and taken to that camp for use there. This action helped establish a fantastic working relationship with the Arlington County Police Department. Whenever I needed some assistance from that agency they were "Johnny on the spot". There were

34 various class rings in lost and found and through some painstaking investigation and research I was able to return all but four of those rings. This was done over a period of months as my primary concern was the investigation of the various incidents, both misdemeanors and felonies that needed my attention. However, this brings to mind some interesting tales concerning these rings.

One ring, a Georgetown University class ring, had been lost for more than twenty-three years. I'm fairly certain that this ring hadn't been in our possession for that amount of time and only God knows where it had been for all those years, but, at any rate it ended up in our lost and found. It took me three days to research the names of graduates for the year indicated on the ring and match the initials inside the ring to the names bearing the same initials. On the third day I was lucky and came up with three names that matched. Now came the task of locating the owner of the ring because in twenty-three years there can be a lot of moving around. With the help of the Alumni Association I was able to obtain addresses for these three people and letters were sent to each one inquiring if any had lost a Georgetown University class ring. Fortunately, the owner called me the following day and described the color of the stone that was mounted in the ring. He couldn't believe that his ring had been found after all these years and arrangements were made to return the ring. About a week after the ring had been returned I was called into Mr. Lamb's office where he presented me with a very nice pen and pencil set that he had received from the owner of the ring along with a very nice letter of appreciation and thanks. I graciously accepted the gift even though I had previously told the owner that I could not accept gratuities for merely doing my job and thanked him for his gesture. I guess that is why he sent the set to Mr. Lamb rather than to me.

While returning another Georgetown University class ring to its owner I discovered that it had been stolen from the owner while staying in a motel in Mobile, Alabama. How it ever ended up in our lost and found is a complete mystery and had I known that it was part of the fruit of a crime I would have taken more handling it so as not to destroy any possible evidence. The owner was a successful attorney who, a couple of years earlier, had been in Alabama on behalf of one of his clients when his room had been broken into, along with several others, and his valuables were stolen. There never was an arrest made in the case and the owner had assumed he would never see his ring again. Upon receiving my letter advising him that I had his ring in my possession he immediately called me and explained the situation.

Inasmuch as he lived near the campus we set a date and time when he could come and retrieve his ring. On that day he appeared at my office carrying a brown paper bag which set on the floor near his chair. I got his ring out of the safe in my office and returned it to a very happy gentleman who produced a smile a mile wide. He then picked up the brown bag and handed it to me and thanked me profusely, however, I had to tell him that I couldn't accept any gifts, but, he became very insistent and at that point Mr. Lamb happened to come into my office. I introduced the owner to Mr. Lamb and the owner explained to Mr. Lamb that he wanted to give me something to show his appreciation. I told the owner that the smile on his face was payment enough; however, Mr. Lamb interceded and said that I could accept his offering. Inside the bag was a fifth bottle of Black and White Scotch and a fifth bottle of Seagram's VO. I thanked the owner and escorted him to his car and just before he got into his car he grabbed me and gave me big bear hug and thanked me again.

There was one ring from a high school in Princeton, New Jersey for which I was able to track the owner. Upon notification of my possession of the ring I was informed by the owner that at that time he was in Europe and wanted to know if one of his relatives could claim it for him. I advised the owner that a relative could do that and he provided me with a name, address, and phone number of the relative. Upon seeing the name of the relative it seemed as though I had come across that name before and when the relative came to my office to claim the ring I recognized the person as a Lieutenant Colonel I had served with when I was I the Air Force. What a chance meeting that was, so, we both sat down and over a couple of cups of coffee we chatted for about a half hour. The Colonel was glad to see that I was doing so well in civilian life and thanked me for returning the ring to his nephew.

One of my first cases involved an armed robbery of the campus book store located at the corner of 37th Street and Prospect Street. The robbery occurred in the day time and what with the location of the book store the perpetrator only had to run across a small parking lot and vanish into the woods adjacent to the campus. The robber had worn a mask making a description of him almost worthless. Officers of the Second District of MPD responded and took a report and referred the case to the Robbery Section. This was the first in a series of armed robberies of the campus book store. In time this case was closed with the arrest of the perpetrator, however, the details of this will come a little later.

During the previous spring break there had been a lot of thefts from the dorm that the basketball team resided in. All these thefts were from rooms that were not occupied by any of the basketball team members and inasmuch as the only student still on campus (with a few exceptions) was the basketball team it certainly would make one a little wary and concerned. The main problem with considering any of them as suspects is the fact that they were the "untouchables". For some strange reason the basketball team was off limits for any type of investigation. This arrangement did not sit well with me and I voiced my concern to the director, however, I was advised that we would discuss this matter at a later time, but, that later time never did materialize. I guess the word got out somehow that there was a new investigator on the campus police department that didn't cut any slack regardless of who you were. At any rate after the Christmas break there were no reports or complaints of any thefts in that particular dorm or any other residence halls.

There had been quite a few reports of thefts in the campus library, so, extra attention was placed in that area and produced several good results. One such case involved a young black male from the District named Victor Alexander. He had been observed taking things out of an unattended purse and the witness reported it to the dispatcher who obtained a description of the suspect and in turn dispatched a couple of officers to that location. After a brief search of the library they apprehended him and brought him to my office for interrogation and additional investigation. Prior to my interviewing the suspect I ran a criminal check on him through MPD and was advised of his criminal history It so happened that there were two phones in my office and one of them was for making calls outside of the campus. The other one was for on campus use and it had a light attached to the side to indicate that someone else was using the outside line. Consequently, if I lifted the handset of the off campus phone, the light on the on campus phone would light up. Also in my office was a red leather arm chair with brass studs all along the edge of the back and on the arms of the chair. Before this suspect was brought to my office I opened a desk drawer and placed the off campus phone inside the drawer where I had access to the handset. Upon his entering my office I advised the suspect of his Miranda rights in the presence of a witness and had him sign and initial a PD Form 47, Miranda Rights Warning. I invited the suspect to have a seat in the red arm chair and after he was seated I told him that was not an ordinary chair. I directed his attention to the little brass studs and advised him that those were connected to various sensors inside the upholstery and could detect if a person was telling the truth or lying.

If a person told a lie the light on the side of the phone which was on my desk would light up. With this bit of information out of the way I proceeded to ask him a few perfunctory questions.

Q: Were you ever arrested before?

A: No. (The light came on as I lifted the handset).

Q: Did you steal anything tonight in the library?

A: No. (The light came on again).

Q: Have you ever committed a burglary?

A: No. (Again the light lit up).

After these questions I informed the suspect that he was lying and that light would keep coming on all night long until he started telling the truth and that things might (and I stressed the word "might") go easier for him to tell the truth. At this point he was thoroughly confused and couldn't figure out how a chair could be a lie detector, but, I had him convinced and he provided a written statement as to his criminal acts on this campus. He also admitted to thefts from other campuses too so the following day I contacted the investigators of the other schools involved and provided them with what information I was able to glean from young Mr. Alexander. I placed Mr. Alexander under arrest and he was transported to the Second District for processing and booking. When the case went to trial he was found guilty of three felony counts and six misdemeanors and was sentenced to several years in prison. With his arrest, confessions and convictions eight different cases were closed.

During my tenure there were numerous very interesting cases that were dealt with. One in particular was when I first met Kevin McCarthy, a detective from Second District (2-D), who ended up being one of my very best friends. As it turned out Kevin and I worked on a lot of cases together. The first one was an alleged robbery on campus that was reported to have happened in one of the dormitory rooms above the McDonough Gymnasium. The dispatcher had received a phone call concerning two students having been tied up and robbed. I responded to the scene and at the same time Detective McCarthy arrived and introduced himself saying that they had monitored the call. After a brief exchange of hand shakes we proceeded to check the alleged robbery scene. I suggested that each of us interview the so called victims separately and then switch off. The interviewing took about ten minutes for each student and their stories were as though someone had written them a script. I suggested to Kevin that we step out into the hallway where I advised him of my thoughts. I think that there was a drug deal that went sour and the students got taken for their money and in order for them to recompense their losses they made up a story of being robbed. It just so happened that Kevin said he was thinking the exact same thing. According to the evidence and the condition of the scene there was nothing to corroborate the complaint. I asked Kevin how he was going to handle this case and he said he was going to file it as unfounded. I agreed and filed my report the same way...UNFOUNDED! Prior to leaving the scene Kevin and I had a discussion within earshot of the two students about the consequences of filing a false police report. You could see the chagrin come over their faces and when we mentioned doing five to ten years in prison I thought they were going to have a cardiac arrest. I believe those two young men learned a very valuable lesson that night without the benefit of having to wear handcuffs. In spite of having developed a certain reputation of being a "hard nose" I was also a very fair person. If I could direct someone on the right path I would and I'd try to do it without creating an unnecessary delinquency record on the person. Once Kevin and I was outside I think we laughed for about five minutes just remembering the expression on their faces when we talked about doing prison time.

There was another time when one of our officers observed two students rolling a keg of beer through parking lot A. When the officer approached them and asked where they got the keg neither one could provide an honest explanation, so, they were brought to the campus police office along with the half keg of beer. They were identified as freshmen students. One of the students, Frank Haas, was extremely mouthy and displayed a complete disregard for authority. I took him into the back area of the offices and laid it on the line with him. I advised him that I didn't particularly like his smart mouth attitude and it could really put him in a very tenuous situation where he could end up with more trouble than he would know what to do with. Unfortunately, he chose to ignore this advice and continued to be a wise guy with a smart mouth. After we returned to the dispatch area he stated that we would all be in deep trouble because the other student involved was Matt Cory, the son of the Governor of New York. I guess that we were supposed to be frightened by this bit of information, so, I thanked him for that knowledge and asked him if he knew the phone number for the governor's mansion to keep me from having to look it up in the phone book. I also asked him for his parent's phone number and that shut him up. It turned out the keg had been taken from the Center Pub, a student operated beer garden on campus. The Pub manager came to the office and positively identified the keg as being theirs; however, inasmuch as he too was a student, he didn't want to go forward with any charges against these two students. Mr. Haas and Mr. Cory were lucky this time, so, we made out field contact cards on them and placed them in our file and then released them with a warning. To me, there's nothing more annoying than a smart mouth punk who thinks he has all the answers and his parents have a lot of influence. They think that influence puts them a few notches above anyone else and authorities can go to hell. Self importance can be a very deadly characteristic.

A student provided me with the name of a possible suspect in the bookstore robberies. Leroy Brown, the suspect, was deeply investigated and as it turned out certain information discovered through the Financial Aid Office revealed that Mr. Brown was indeed a prison inmate who had been convicted of four bank robberies and was attending Georgetown University under some type of educational release program. Further investigation revealed that there was one other student inmate in the same program. I advised my director of these developments and I thought he was going to have a stroke…he immediately called the Dean of Student Affairs and asked if he knew about these two students and their backgrounds. Apparently there very few people on the campus that was aware of these two students in particular our department. There's an old saying "if a snake is under your chair it's good to know about it" and that is the situation with this case. Robert Johnson, the other prison inmate maintained his grades and did not get into any trouble, so, he was merely monitored for a while and then cleared of any wrong doing or any involvement in these robberies. Additional investigation provided enough evidence to obtain an arrest warrant for Mr. Brown; however, he had left the campus a few days earlier and had not attended any of his classes. Apparently he was aware that we knew of his actions and were after him, so, the MPD was advised of the warrant, and all pertinent information pertaining to Mr. Brown was released to them along with a recent photo of him. The hunt for Brown continued for almost two weeks when one of the female students who knew him contacted our office and advised my investigator, Sylvester Julian, that she had just seen Mr. Brown on a street corner in midtown D.C. Sylvester made arrangements to meet the girl and immediately left for their rendezvous. Upon their meeting she showed Sylvester where the suspect was and being unarmed Sylvester solicited the aid of Officer Nick Demiduck who happened to be patrolling that particular area. Officer Demiduck was advised of the outstanding warrant and that the suspect might possibly be armed. The suspect at this time was standing at a bus stop as Officer Demiduck came up behind him with his service weapon drawn and placed the barrel in the suspects back advising him to raise both hands and not to do anything stupid. Sylvester assisted Officer Demiduck place the suspect in handcuffs and upon being searched pursuant to the arrest a loaded .25 caliber hand gun was found in one of his pockets. Mr. Brown was read his Miranda Rights and transported to the Second District Headquarters where he again was Mirandized and interrogated by me, Sylvester and 2-D Detectives. Mr. Brown provided a written statement where he admitted committing the bookstore robberies along with several other robberies not connected to the university. It was a good days work and I submitted a commendation for Sylvester for his quick action as I was on another assignment at the time this all took place. After Mr. Brown's trial he was found guilty of several counts of armed robbery and sentenced to a total of thirty five years plus having to finish the time he was doing for the previous bank robberies. Yes sir, it was a good day's work!

A few months after this incident, besides all the other cases we were working on, the manager of the East Campus Bookstore, located at 36th and N Street, NW, reported that her car had been stolen. I responded to her location and took down all the necessary information and advised MPD of the situation. Officers of the Second

District met with me and an LOF (Look Out For) was transmitted to all units with a description of the vehicle. It wasn't long before we got a call stating that the vehicle had been recovered and there two suspects in custody. When I arrived at 2D Headquarters I saw Frank Haas and Matt Cory sitting in one of the holding cells. Ah yes, revenge is sweet. The big mouth finally got to feel what it was like sitting in a jail cell, but, he still had that attitude that his friends' dad, the Governor, would get them out of trouble again. Both of the students were processed and charged with Unauthorized Use of a Vehicle (UUV) and transported down to the D.C. Central Cell Block to await arraignment. In all honesty, I would rather spend six months in Sing Sing rather than one night in the Central Cell Block of the D.C. jail. After the case was papered in the U. S. Attorney's Office we just had to sit back and wait for a trial date. It was during this time that the complainant, Mrs. Rosie Daniels, got a visit from two detectives from the New York State Police practically begging her to withdraw her complaint, but, God bless her, she held her ground and told them they'd be better off back in New York. After these two detectives left her store she contacted me and told me all about her visit from these two men. I advised her that should they return to call me immediately. These two detectives didn't want to take no for an answer, so, the following day they came back to plead with her again and she told them she'd have to think about it and for them to come back in an hour for her decision. Again she called me and I in turn called the 2D Detectives and spoke to Kevin McCarthy and related to him what was going on. In a matter of minutes Kevin was in my office and as the time drew near for the return of the men from New York we proceeded to the East Campus Bookstore to wait for them. It wasn't a very long wait before they entered the store and again tried to speak with Mrs. Daniels. At this point Kevin and I approached them and identified ourselves and requested some identification from them at which point they produced their shield and photo ID Cards. In no uncertain terms we advised them that it would be in their best interest to return to their car and head back to New York as fast as possible or they would be arrested for harassment and trying to influence a complaining witness. They were also advised that the reason they're not being arrested at this time was due to professional courtesy and if any more attempts were made to contact the complainant a federal warrant will be obtained for their arrest. With that said they departed the store, got into their car, and were followed all the way to the Baltimore-Washington Parkway by a marked patrol car. Before the case ever came to trial the parents of both boys took them out of school. When their case did go to trial, because of their age and this being their first time in trouble with the law, they were given first offender status whereas they were to stay out of trouble for one year and their criminal record would be expunged. To be honest with you I think there might have been a certain amount of influence and discretion on the part of the judge for handing down such a soft sentence, but, as the saying goes "you can't fight city hall!" At least I could go to sleep at night with a clear conscious knowing that I did the right thing. Of course, being a father myself, I guess I can understand the governor's actions.

Then there was the case of two female students that came to my office to report the theft of personal items including their credit cards from their off campus apartment. They also even provided the name of a possible suspect…Sue Anderson, another female student who had been invited to their apartment on several occasions. The two complainants weren't aware of these thefts until they got their credit card monthly statements and saw a lot of purchases that they never made. In addition to their credit cards being stolen their Riggs Bank ATM cards were taken also and used for withdrawals. I contacted Jim Johnson, the head of Riggs Bank Security and met with him and explained the situation. Jim was extremely helpful and allowed us (me and the complainants) to view the video tapes of the M Street branch for the dates indicated on their bank statement when the withdrawals were made. On all these tapes the image of the same girl appeared. Jim provided me with photos from all the tapes where she appeared and the tapes included the dates and time of the transactions. This gave me probable cause to bring the suspect in for questioning. I read the girl her Miranda Rights with a female officer present and had the officer stay in the room during the interview to preclude any possible future charges of misconduct or mistreatment on my part. As expected the girl denied any wrong doing and stated that she came from a wealthy background with no need to steal and insisted that I had the wrong person, however, when confronted with the photos from the tapes she broke down and the tears started falling like rain. She confessed to everything. The cash withdrawals from the bank, the numerous purchases she had made at Nieman and Marcus, Blumenthal's, Hecht's, and the Galleria. When asked why she did these things she couldn't give a reasonable answer. The complainants were not vindictive and didn't necessarily want her arrested, but, they didn't want her to go without some form of punishment. Sue was extremely fortunate in this case as she faced being charged with seven felonies and quite a few misdemeanors. It was agreed upon by the complainants to have her tried by Student Adjudication. This convening authority is primarily made up of students with a few faculty members as advisers. There have been cases brought before them where the defendant received a much harsher punishment than what he/she would have received in a criminal court in DC. In Sue's case she was ordered to make full restitution to the two complainants in addition to being suspended from school for the remainder of the semester which had barely started when this incident occurred. She was further directed to seek psychological help as she couldn't explain why she committed these actions.

The Center Pub, which is operated solely by students, is a natural gathering place. They had a DJ and dance floor, three different brands of beer, and a kitchen area where they made pizzas. They sold various brands of cigarettes and had waiter/waitress service. During the Easter break Bob Mahoney, the Pub Manager, appeared at my office and advised that the Pub had been broken into and things were missing. I responded to the Pub and investigated and dusted for fingerprints from various areas. Bob provided a list of missing property which consisted of an eight foot by two foot wooden sign that had "GEORGETOWN

UNIVERSITY CENTER PUB" inscribed on it, several cartons of various brands of cigarettes, and numerous LP record albums taken from the DJ booth. Inasmuch as all the students, with the exception for a few, were gone for the Easter break there wasn't too much that could be accomplished, however, as I was sitting down for dinner on Easter Sunday I received a phone call from Jerry Mercouri, the DJ at the Pub. He gave me the name of a possible suspect in the break in (actually it is officially classified as a Burglary II). I queried him as to why he thought this student was involved and he informed me that the students' roommate told him that the suspect had a lot of cigarettes in his bureau drawers. In view of this information I made a few phone calls from my home and obtained verbal permission to conduct a search of the suspect's room with the paper work to be completed the following business day and I immediately departed for the campus. Upon my arrival I had two uniformed officers accompany me to the dorm room. I knocked on the door and was somewhat surprised when the suspect, Joseph Randherst, opened the door. I produced my badge and identified myself and advised him that I had a warrant to search his room for contraband from a crime that occurred on campus. I looked in all the nooks and crannies with no signs of the sign or the LP's. I noticed a bureau drawer partially open that contained a lot of cigarettes. I advised Joseph to open that drawer all the way and as he did I could see that it was stuffed with different brands of cigarettes. I read Joe the Miranda Warning and asked him if there was anything he wanted to say at that time, to which, he admitted taking part in the burglary. At that point I had him taken to my office in the O'Gara Building where I conducted a further interrogation. After a period of time Joe became pretty cooperative (especially after I advised him that he was looking at a possible 3 to 5 years in prison for Burglary II) and he gave up the other two students involved, Matt English and Peter Burrows. Both English and Burrows were away from the campus on Easter break so everything was placed on hold until their return. At this point it should be noted that the university, under the *in loco parentis* Act, has the authority, upon probable cause, to search student's residence hall rooms providing it is accomplished by an authorized campus official. These searches have been upheld also in the DC criminal courts when various crimes had been referred to those courts for disposition. In those particular cases though if an outside law enforcement agency such as MPD or the FBI is involved with the search that renders the search invalid. Upon their return to campus, English and Burrows were brought to my office where they were advised of their rights under Miranda and interrogated separately. I told them that I knew all about their actions at the Center Pub and demanded the return of the stolen items. I also advised them that their actions constituted an act of Burglary II which is punishable by 3 to 5 years imprisonment. With this knowledge, they both admitted their respective parts in the crime and promised to return the property immediately. I obtained written statements from all three of the suspects and discussed the prosecution options with Mr. Lamb. It was decided to submit this case to Student Adjudication and two weeks later they were brought up before the adjudication board. I presented the case for the university and, in view of the seriousness of the charges against them; they had all gotten attorneys to represent them. This hearing started at 7:00 o'clock p.m. and lasted for approximately three hours and then the deliberation of the panel lasted another two hours. Around midnight we were all summoned back into the hearing room where the board members rendered their decision. Based upon the preponderance of the evidence submitted and their written statements, all three students were found guilty and sentenced to suspension for two years from school, full restitution for any losses or damages, and a written apology to the employees of the Center Pub. Downtown in court they would have received first offender status which would have been a slap on the wrist and probably an admonition from the judge telling them they were bad boys. All stolen property had been returned to the Pub. Joseph Randhurst and Peter Burrows never did return to Georgetown after their suspension was over. Matt English returned and came to my office and told me that he harbored no hard feelings toward me and thanked me for taking the case to Student Adjudication rather than criminal court. On the brighter side of this case, Matt had learned a very important lesson and four years after graduating from Georgetown University he graduated from Georgetown University Law School.

Somehow, somewhere down the line it became a school tradition to steal the hands from the clock in Healy Tower. To begin with, this is a very, very high clock tower and in order to get to the clock mechanism you have to go through a series of doors on various floor levels and then climb the stairs to the upper reaches of the tower. Additionally, you have to traverse through three or four inches of pigeon droppings. Needless to say this is an extremely dangerous endeavor...but, some moronic students take the challenge every year. Fortunately no one has fallen to their death because of being overly stupid and in the interest of safety I was directed to explore the various means of access and submit recommendations to ensure no further attempts would be successful. This was all brought about after the last theft of the hands occurred. Through information I had obtained from a couple of informants I was able to identify the person responsible for this last theft of the clock hands, a freshman named William Everest. I had him escorted to my office where he was advised of his Miranda rights even though he wasn't placed under arrest. He decided to be cooperative and agreed to show me how he had gained access to the clock tower and remove the clock hands. This was a very circuitous route which required us to climb an external fire escape to the roof of the Jesuit Community which was the equivalent of six stories. Then we had to crawl along the edge of this roof to where the Jesuit Community and the Healy Building connect. There was a triangular shaped trap door on the roof there that we opened and then lowered ourselves down to ceiling beams which we had to walk across to get to where access could be made to the third floor attic of the Healy Building. Once inside this attic we then had to pry open another door to the stairs to get to the fourth floor attic. From there we proceeded to the stairs going up into the clock tower itself. At this point I had wished I'd known what to expect...the smell was overwhelming and apparently at one time this attic had been used for some sort of occult ritual as a couple of pigeons had been hung by their necks and there were some sort of pentagrams and occult symbols drawn on the floor. After our little trek to the far reaches of Healy Tower we returned to my office where I obtained a written statement from William. He also told me what he had done with the clock hands…he sent them to the President of the United States. In view of this I made contact with the Secret Service and was directed to the person in charge of all White House incoming mail and packages. I explained to this person what the situation was and after looking for about a half hour they found the clock hands still in their opened packaging. The hands were returned to me after I signed all kinds of release forms and I returned to the university. The Physical Plant Department, responsible for replacing the hands was contacted and someone from that department came and retrieved them. I did have the courtesy to inform them that when they went up to replace the clock hands to wear old clothes that they no longer wanted and take along some type of respirator so they wouldn't be overcome by the stench. In view of the cooperation given by William I did recommend some leniency in his punishment. For that he was grateful and for the remainder of his time at Georgetown he didn't present any problems. With the closure of this incident, my recommendations to secure the clock hands were submitted and within a week they were acted on.

I guess Georgetown University doesn't stand alone when it comes to dishonest employees. As a matter of fact I recall the case of the President of American University being alleged as the person responsible for making obscene phone calls to female students...see what an education can do for you.

There was one particular employee of the Housekeeping Department, Larry Hale, whose name frequently came to my attention involving thefts. One day I received a phone call from Detective Dave Roberts, 2D Pawn Shop Detail asking if we had an employee by the name of Larry Hale to which I replied yes and that I'd had my eye on him for quite some time. Dave told me I should come to his office as he had something that would be of great interest to me. Prior to this call there had been a report filed a few days earlier of the theft of numerous band instruments. Upon my arrival to Dave's office he showed the daily printout of the various pawn shop activities and Larry's name was listed as pawning a whole lot of musical instruments. Dave provided me with copies of these documents and I returned to the O'Gara Building and discussed the matter with Mr. Lamb. It looked like we finally had enough on Larry Hale to put him away for quite some time, but, after speaking with the person in charge of the band instruments all thoughts of this happening went down the proverbial tubes. No one had bothered to neither record the serial numbers off the instruments nor put any identifying marks on them to prove that they belonged to the university. Here was a perfectly excellent case to go to trial with and just because of someone's negligence (or ignorance) the perpetrator was let off the hook. In the District of Columbia all pawn shops are required to demand photo identification of persons when they pawn an item and record this information on specific forms that are then submitted daily to the Metropolitan Police Department. This information is then disseminated daily to all seven police districts.

Larry's luck had finally run its course because a month or so later I received another call from Dave Roberts advising that Larry's name has shown up again on another pawn shop report. This time it was for a Nikon 35mm camera. I researched our burglary and theft reports and found several complainants of camera thefts. Thank God for the ability of our officers when taking a report and recording the serial numbers of the stolen items when available. I found the report I was looking for and advised Dave that I would make a copy for him. That afternoon I met with Dave and we prepared an affidavit in support of a search warrant and went downtown to the superior court and had it signed by a judge, recorded and a warrant issued for the search of Larry Hale's residence, person, and other property under his control. This search couldn't have been more fruitful as we recovered numerous Georgetown University class rings, various high school class rings, cameras, binoculars, empty wallets with identification cards for various persons other than Larry Hale. Why he would keep these wallets is beyond my wildest imagination. Oh yeah, we found a few musical instruments too that he hadn't gotten around to pawn. Larry was placed under arrest at his home and taken to 2D for booking and interrogation. Needless to say he was terminated from Georgetown University and later when his case came before the Grand Jury there were twenty seven witnesses that testified against him. The Grand Jury returned a true bill (indictment) charging Larry Hale with thirty five felonies and thirty three misdemeanors. This was the last of Larry Hale on this campus, but, I advised the investigators of all the other universities and colleges in the consortium and they screened their files and several of them came up with cases against Larry. It took a long time coming, but, justice finally found its way to Larry's front door.

To a cop there is nothing worse than a dirty cop. Practically all police departments, no matter how small or large has at least one or two. We were not exempt. There had been several thefts from offices and unlocked residence hall rooms over a period of about three weeks. During one particular theft a Riggs Bank card was taken and used at the ATM of Riggs Bank on M Street and Wisconsin Avenue. I contacted my friend at Riggs Bank Security, Jim Johnson, and the complainant and I proceeded to his office. Jim was just as helpful as before and provided us with all the documentation we would need to prosecute this case. Upon returning to my office I conferred with Mr. Lamb as to how he wanted this case handled inasmuch as it was one of our officers who was the suspect and whose face appeared on the photo from the bank records. Mr. Lamb said to do what I thought proper, so, I had the dispatcher radio for Officer Tom Simmons to return back to the station. Upon his arrival he was directed to my office where I had him close the door and have a seat. I advised him of his Miranda rights and then told him what some of the evidence against him was. He swore he had nothing to do with any of the thefts, but, when confronted with the photo from the bank he immediately became mute. I had him surrender his shield and ID card and placed him under arrest. I escorted him to the locker room where he changed out of uniform while waiting for a transport officer from Second District to arrive to take Simmons in for booking. During interrogation Simmons admitted to several of the thefts and then was transferred to the Central Cell Block downtown. During the remainder of my tenure at Georgetown there was never another case of any of our officers going bad.

At the end of the school year the university would contract with various housekeeping companies to come to the campus and clean all the residence halls and apartments. This is the period of time known as "Senior Week" as the only students remaining on campus are the graduating seniors. All week long there are parties, special events for the students and tons of activities. This also is the time when the contract housekeeping cleaners are performing their respective chores. It is also a time when numerous valuable items seem to disappear. One such case occurred in May and involved a contract cleaner who was arrested by one of our officer's on the day the Law School was having their graduation. The suspect, Neil Burns, lived in Baltimore, Maryland where his company was located. Their cleaning crews were bussed down and back every day from Baltimore. On this particular day the suspect was observed coming out of an apartment in Village

B where he had no business of being there. He was questioned by our officers for his presence in that area and being unable to provide a reasonable answer for being there he was placed under arrest for Unlawful Entry, transported to Second District, and processed. About one week later I had received a call from a Sergeant Tom Richardson of the Baltimore City Police advising that he had in his possession a Canon camera with a case and several lenses. He had taken the camera from a black male who was attempting to pawn it. Sergeant Richardson had the film inside developed in an attempt to determine the owner and there were pictures showing a Georgetown University banner, so, he was checking to see if we had any reported thefts of a camera matching that description. I got his phone number and advised that I would search our records and get back to him. Our records reflected three complainants and each one was contacted and questioned about their losses. All three victims were able to provide me with serial numbers of their cameras and when I called Sgt Richardson back and relayed the information to him he stated that he had a match and could I come to Baltimore with the victim for positive identification of the camera and its contents. Inasmuch as Detective Ron Verwers of Second District was also working this case I advised him of these new developments. Ron made arrangements for the transportation and met with me and the victim the following morning and we proceeded to Baltimore. There the complainant, James Craig, made positive identification of the camera plus describing the various activities reflected in the photos. He also provided the serial numbers for the lenses. The camera was returned to Mr. Craig and upon our return to D.C. I prepared an affidavit in support of an arrest warrant. The following morning I proceeded to Superior Court where I had the affidavit signed by the Judge-in-Chambers, had it recorded and a warrant was issued for the arrest of Neil Burns for Burglary II. In June, Neil Burns had to appear in Superior Court on the charge of Unlawful Entry. Inasmuch as Burns lived in Baltimore he didn't have any criminal history in the District, consequently, he was given first offender status and released. Prior to him leaving the courtroom Detective Verwers and I left the courtroom and waited in the hall for Mr. Burns. As he exited the courtroom I said hello to him and asked how everything was going to which he replied "beautiful". He was just as happy as a lark and here I had to go and ruin his day. I advised him he was under arrest for Burglary II and for him to grab a handful of wall and assume the position. Detective Verwers placed the handcuffs on him and we escorted him from the building and he was taken to Second District. During the interrogation he admitted to several other thefts and gave up the names of three other contract cleaners that were thieves also. Armed with this information I advised Mr. Lamb and recommended that their contract be voided. Before the day had ended a back up cleaning company was contracted and the current cleaner's contract was voided and they were advised that if anyone of them returns to this campus they would be arrested for unlawful entry.

In view of these incidents I suggested that in the future all prospective contractors must provide a list of their employees that would be working on this campus and the list must contain the complete names, dates of birth and social security numbers. This list would then be run through NCIC (National Criminal Information Center) to check for any criminal records of the proposed personnel. Those found to have a criminal record would not be allowed to be on this campus. Needless to say, of the lists provided, more than twenty five percent of the listed personnel had criminal records ranging from petty theft to burglary and robbery. This is a prime example of the saying "it's hard to find good help".

Unfortunately, it wasn't only the contract cleaner's that had thieves amongst them…our own housekeeping department had several too other than Larry Hale. In the basement hall of Healy Building there were several vending machines and game machines. At this point it should be noted that in the District the breaking and entering of a vending machine is classified as a felony as opposed to being a misdemeanor. There was one particular period of time where theft from these machines was almost an everyday occurrence. There were no visible signs of forced entry and it became a mystery as to how these thefts were occurring. In view of this situation it was determined that surveillance would be required, but, there really wasn't a suitable location to establish a surveillance post. Consequently, a hidden surveillance camera disguised as an emergency lighting system was rented and installed where it covered all the vending machines. The only problem with this type of camera was that the film in it had to be replaced every other day and it was extremely hard to do without giving it away as a camera. To overcome this set back it was decided to shut the Healy Basement down at 2:00am for the "exterminator's" to treat the area. That was when I would make the film change and then later in the morning I would take the film to be developed. It only took three days of using the camera to get our desired results. The pictures showed just as clear as if you were standing next to the machines three housekeeping men at 4:26am turning the machines upside down and shaking them until all the coins came out onto the floor. It sounds like a dumb thing to do and a lot of trouble to go to just for some "chump change", but, there it was in black and white. I now had probable cause to obtain arrest warrants for all three of these guy's, so, I prepared the affidavits, took them downtown to have them processed and came back to the campus with the arrest warrants in my hand. Prior to these housekeepers leaving for the day I was told by their supervisor where they were working, so, with assistance of one of my other investigator's, Charlie Adkins, we proceeded to each job site and, one at a time, placed the individuals under arrest, handcuffed them and led away in public view so others would get the message. It is extremely embarrassing to be led off your job in handcuffs with everyone watching and that is exactly the point I wanted to make.

There was an office in Healy Basement that was used by the Student Corp. a student run mini market in the basement and there had been reports of money being stolen from an unlocked safe in that office. The way this office was laid out consisted of actually two offices, one inner office and the outer office. We obtained one hundred and ten dollars from the Student Corp. for bait money. I opted for that amount in the event this venture was successful it would constitute a felony. In my office we recorded the serial numbers and dusted this money with theft detection powder and placed it in an unmarked, unsealed envelope. The following morning at about 4:00am, I and my partner, Assistant Director Jeff Horton, proceeded to this office and placed the envelope inside the unlocked safe, closed the door partially and then we waited in the inner office. At about 6:30am we heard someone enter the outer office and we heard a vacuum cleaner being run. We were able to see the safe in the outer office through a crack in the door and when the cleaner noise stopped I was able to observe the cleaning lady assigned to clean these offices walk out into the hallway. As soon as she left the office we checked the safe and discovered that the envelope was missing. We immediately approached the cleaning lady, identified ourselves and showed her our badges and escorted her back to the offices. I asked her if she had just cleaned the Student Corp. office and she admitted that she had. I then asked her to empty all of her pockets and place the contents on top of the desk in the office. Among the items placed on the desk was the treated money. I asked her where she got the money and she stated that she brought it to work with her so she could stop on the way home for groceries. I put on a pair of surgical gloves and took out the sheet of paper with the serial numbers of the baited money.

As Jeff read off the numbers I checked them off the list and then we placed Millie Bates under arrest for Theft I (theft in excess of $100.00). During this process, Millie had perspired somewhat and I advised her to look at her hands. When she saw how her hands were stained with a deep purple color dye she realized that she had been caught for good and wanted to make a deal by providing information on other thefts that were still open cases. By the way, for those not familiar with theft detection powder, it doesn't wash off. In time it will fade and disappear, but, until it does, every time a thief looks at his/her hands they wonder why in the world were they so stupid to steal. The information Millie gave us was pretty helpful and I advised Mike Hull, the Assistant U.S. Attorney that Millie had been cooperative with us and he made a note of that in his papers.

There was another time when a cigarette vending machine had been broken into and one of the students saw the person and advised me who it was. I knew the man who worked in the housekeeping department, so, I and Detective John J. Kerrigan who just happened to be in my office at the time the student came to see me, proceeded to the housekeeping office and had the supervisor call George Carson to her office. Upon George's arrival I told him I knew what he had done and asked him what he did with the cigarettes from the machine. Naturally, George said he didn't have a clue as to what I was talking about, so, I informed him that I had enough evidence and an eye witness to get an arrest warrant and it would go twice as bad for him if I had to resort to that. Consequently, George took us to his locker and surrendered two big brown paper bags full of cigarettes. At that point George was placed under arrest and given his Miranda rights, but, when we attempted to place the handcuffs on him his wrists were so big none of them would fit. This is when John told him that he would be transported to Second District without handcuffs, but, any sudden hostile movement or attempt to flee would require John to shoot him. George's eyes got as big as saucers and sweat started coming out of his pores like Niagara Falls. George stated that there wouldn't be any problems with him and the transport went smoothly. After I got off work that evening I went to a local police equipment store, the "Cop Shop" in Arlington, Virginia and made the purchase of a set of thumb cuffs just so I wouldn't get caught short again without some sort of restraining device.

There had been another series of vending machines being broken into at the Medical School cafeteria. It was during this time when we had a lot of construction for a helicopter landing pad being done in that area and the construction workers would make use of the cafeteria at lunch time and during their breaks. By some strange coincidence this was the time of day when the machines were discovered to have been broken into, so, I proceeded to the construction company trailer and talked with the site supervisor in an attempt to garner what information I could that might be of some help. I was advised that one of his employees had been spending an inordinate amount of time in the cafeteria and had been reprimanded for it on a couple of occasions. I got all the necessary information about this subject and ran his name through NCIC to determine if he had a criminal record and sure enough he had one for various offenses, one of which was breaking and entering vending machines. In view of this knowledge and information received from several of the cafeteria workers describing this subject as a white male with purple splotches on his face. I returned to the construction trailer on the very day that one of the machines had been hit. Upon my arrival at the trailer the subject was not at the site and the supervisor had no idea where he might be. I gave my business card to the supervisor and requested that he call me as soon as the subject returned. I also asked him to keep the subject at his location until I arrived. While I was in my office typing the report on this case I got a phone call from the supervisor that the subject was back at the site. I immediately proceeded to that location and upon seeing the subject I noticed that his front pockets were bulging with something. In the presence of the site supervisor and site foreman I identified myself to the subject and advised him that he was a suspect in numerous thefts from vending machines and I instructed him to empty all of his pockets and place the contents on an empty table that was in the office. After emptying his pockets I saw there was a tremendous amount of silver American currency, mostly quarters, dimes and nickels. Almost all these coins bore the traces of the theft detection powder that had been applied to them prior to being placed in the machine earlier with a sign taped to the machine stating that it was out of order. Based on this evidence and the fact that his hands also were stained from the powder I placed the subject under arrest, handcuffed him, and gave him his Miranda warning. While waiting for the transport officer from Second District to arrive he became quite talkative and after our arrival at Second District while he was being interrogated by me and Detective Bud Haley, he volunteered to show us how he managed to get into the machines with a fingernail clipper. All three of us proceeded to the vending machine room at the Second District station and in less time than it took to open the machine with a key the suspect had it opened and displayed the coin box. Bud and I couldn't believe how fast he did that. To put the icing on the cake, a few months later we were in Superior Court for his trial. During a lunch recess he approached me in the hallway, said hello and asked if I had change for a dollar. I told him that I didn't and he went on his way. About an hour later as Bud and I were in the hallway waiting for the trial to resume the defendant, Walter Pierce, came up to us and showed us his bulging pockets and said "I've got plenty of change now". We couldn't believe it…this guy hit another vending machine during lunch break. I immediately went inside the courtroom and spoke to the Assistant U. S. Attorney (AUSA) that was trying the case and advised him of these new developments. I thought he was going to fall all over the floor laughing. Inasmuch as we were not allowed in the courtroom until being called as a witness we had no idea what was taking place inside, but, as it turned out we didn't have to testify and the AUSA told us that he had gotten a conviction on fifteen counts of breaking and entering vending machines. That is a lot of time in prison out of a young man's life.

After receiving numerous complaints of thefts from rooms of a certain area of Village C, one of the new residence halls, we gave that area special attention and interviewed the complainants at great lengths. Based on the information we had obtained it was determined that most of these thefts occurred after there had been some type of maintenance performed in the room. I contacted Lou Lieberman, Supervisor of the Physical Plant Department, to determine who had been assigned work orders for any repairs to be done in that area. Lou advised me that his employees were assigned certain areas of responsibility and gave me the name of the employee assigned to this area, James Dobson. With this information I again contacted my contact at Second District and ran a criminal check on Mr. Dobson. The only thing on his record was a couple of DUI's (Driving under the Influence), but nothing criminal in nature. I decided to do a "sting operation" in one of those rooms to test the honesty of Mr. Dobson. I took out two twenty dollar bills from petty cash, recorded the serial numbers, and dusted them with theft detection powder. I placed this money in an old wallet and contacted the room occupant to come to my office. This student was advised that there was an ongoing criminal investigation and she was requested to contact me when she left her room the next morning. She was also requested not to return to her room until she first talked to me to which she agreed. The following morning after I received her call of leaving the room I had one of our female officers call the maintenance help desk to complain about a running toilet in that particular room. While this call was being made one of my investigators, Charlie Adkins, proceed to that room and place the "bait wallet" inside the drawer of the bedside table, but, leaving the drawer open enough that the wallet could be easily seen. After the call was completed I met with Charlie in Village C and as I maintained surveillance on the room Charlie established another location where he would have immediate access to the room once the maintenance person had left. After about an hour of waiting a maintenance person entered the room and ten minutes later departed. Charlie immediately went into the room and discovered that the wallet was still there, but, the money was gone. Charlie radioed this information to me and as the maintenance person approached me I stopped him, identified myself and showed him my shield and advised him to accompany me into the residence hall lounge. Charlie met with us a couple minutes later and with him there as a witness I advised the maintenance person, James Dobson, that he was a suspect in thefts from dorm rooms and I instructed him to empty out his pockets and place everything on a table in the lounge. Among the items from his pockets were the two twenty dollar bills with the theft detection powder on them. The serial numbers matched those that we had recorded and the suspect was placed under arrest for Burglary II and advised of his Miranda Rights. In addition to this evidence, Mr. Dobson's hands were deeply stained purple from the powder. We all proceeded to my office where I prepared the necessary paper work involved pursuant to an arrest while waiting for a transport unit from Second District. In the mean time, the father of the suspect, also an employee in Physical Plant came storming into my office ranting and raving and demanding that his son be set free. At this point I informed Frank Dobson that if he didn't get himself under control he too would be locked up for Disorderly Conduct. After a few minutes Frank finally settled down and realized that I meant business and I was in no mood for any craziness. I advised Frank of the evidence we had against his son and told him that it was a good lawful arrest, however, he countered with the accusation of entrapment. I explained to Frank the elements of entrapment and that it didn't apply in this case. I also suggested that he get his son a good attorney and he might be able to get off with first offender status inasmuch as he has no prior criminal history. Before the transport unit arrived I allowed Frank to talk with his son before he left the office. Shortly thereafter the transport unit arrived and took James Dobson to Second District where he was booked for Burglary II. For some unexplained reason

Frank Dobson never spoke to me again after that day and you can't imagine how much that depressed me.

(Perhaps at this point the differences between Burglary I and Burglary II should be explained. Burglary I is a crime where person(s) enter or break and enter a dwelling or building with the purpose of committing a crime while the dwelling or building is being occupied by human being(s). Burglary II is the same set of circumstances with the exception of no occupants involved.)

As you might have perceived by now, Georgetown University is pretty much self sustaining. It has its own Riggs Bank branch office, U. S. Post Office, The Center Pub, a mini mart which was always well stocked, a snack shack, a student credit union, and a Student Corporation Council who has the responsibility to oversee all these ventures. I have to give these students a lot of credit to operate these enterprises as successfully as they did. Of course, as in all businesses, there is going to be some sort of problem. Such was the case with the mini mart. On various occasions their nightly deposits didn't exactly coincide with the cash intake for those particular days. I conducted interviews with all persons working in the mini mart that had access to the money and or was involved with any of the deposits. Everyone appeared to be free from any wrong doing, but, I knew there was someone that was responsible for these inconsistencies. After two days of going over the various work schedules and hours worked by each employee the field was narrowed down to four persons. Each of these students was interrogated at great lengths. Patricia Wells, after about an hour and a half of being questioned finally broke down and confessed. She had been embezzling from the Corp for almost five months in the amount of well over $10,000. Patricia was not from a real wealthy family and had a boyfriend that depended on her for spending money. She had treated them both to trips to Las Vegas and Florida and she even bought him expensive jewelry such as watches and rings and bracelets. Her boyfriend was not a student, so, he was out of our jurisdiction, but, I passed his name to my detective friends at Second District and other MPD officers just as a matter of courtesy to them. Naturally, Patricia was placed under arrest and she was accompanied to her bank where she withdrew what was left of the stolen money and we returned to my office. I made out a receipt for this money ($1,348) and placed it in an evidence envelope and placed the envelope in the safe in my office. I requested a female officer from Second District for a transport of Patricia. While we were waiting for the transport officer to arrive, Patricia asked to make a phone call to her mother to which I agreed. I knew this was a very hard call for her to make, but, her mother would have found out about it sooner or later and it was best that the news came from Patricia. During this phone conversation her mother asked to speak to me. Understandably Mrs. Wells was in tears and extremely upset, so, I did my best to calm her and just let her vent all her frustrations. Mrs. Wells had no hard feelings toward me and accepted the fact that I was doing my job and it was her daughters own fault for being in the trouble she was in. I make it a habit not to get personally involved with my cases; however, in this incident I did make an exception and assisted Mrs. Wells as much as I possibly could as she had to come all the way from Maine by herself. Patricia was arraigned the following day and inasmuch as she was a student with no risk of flight she was released on her own recognizance until her trial date. In the end, Patricia pled guilty rather than have a jury trial and the judge sentenced her to full restitution, one year imprisonment (suspended) and two years of probation and court costs. Of course, it goes without saying that she was also expelled from Georgetown University. All in all, I think Patricia made out alright considering everything.

During the mid term exams we had an incident one day at around 2:00pm in one of the men's room in the

Reiss Science Building where a student had gone off the wall and totally trashed the place. The student, Jonathan Martin, was apprehended at the scene and brought to my office. It was apparent that Jonathan had been doing some heavy drinking of alcohol or beer and was completely incoherent. I suggested to my boss that the student be given the opportunity to sleep it off as it would be fruitless to try to talk to him in his present state of mind. Mr. Lamb agreed and we placed him in our holding cell where he could lie down and get himself in order. About 5:30pm Jonathan woke up not knowing where he was or how he had gotten here. I brought him into my office where we both had a cup of coffee and inasmuch as Jonathan was a freshman and his first time away from home I more or less acted like a "Dutch Uncle" to him. We chatted for a while and I got around to asking him why he tore up the men's room like he did. Jonathan had absolutely no idea what I was talking about and at first I thought this was going to be one of those "…it must have been amnesia" dodges. It turned out that I was wrong about that and that he really didn't know what he had done, so, I took him to the men's room to show him the damage, and he couldn't believe his eyes. As it turned out the reason for doing what he had done was because he had gotten a B+ on one of his mid term exams. I asked him what was so terrible about that…I'd be tickled to death to get a grade like that. He replied that the grade didn't bother him so much as it would his father. Jonathan had maintained straight A's all the way through school and even at Georgetown all of his grades were A's with this one exception. When he saw that grade he said he just lost it and went on a drinking binge even though he had never tasted any alcoholic beverages in his life (all eighteen years of it). He got very depressed and even had thoughts of suicide because of what his father would think and do. In view of this I contacted the Dean of Students and requested an appointment for myself and Jonathan. The next morning I met with Jonathan at my office and we proceeded to the Dean's office. We explained to the Dean what the situation was as far as his father and his grades and what had happened the day before. The Dean was very compassionate and advised that he would take care of matters and I could turn the case over to him. Prior to leaving the Dean's office I gave Jonathan a reassuring pat on the shoulder and told him everything was going to be alright. Everything did turn out okay too. Jonathan was made to pay for the repairs to the damaged men's room and his father received a very tactful suggestion that he should not place too much emphasis on Jonathan's grades rather than on Jonathan himself. Good grades are nice to have, but, not to the point where it is the most important thing in the world. Life is too short to get ulcers over an outstanding grade point average (GPA). Ever since that episode whenever I would see Jonathan he would always smile and wave "hello". Even after he graduated, he would send me a Christmas card every December. He was a very grateful young man and I don't have a clue as to where he is today, but, wherever he is and whatever he may be doing I'm sure he is very successful at it.

Another student had a different way of trying to get a good grade on a mid term exam. I will say that he put a lot of thought into his plan and it almost worked except for a little thing like a fire that got out of control.

Jerry Thomas produced a letter to his professor from a doctor in New Jersey advising that Jerry had a very important doctor's appointment on the same day that the mid term exam was to be taken for one of his science courses. In view of this Jerry asked his professor if he could take the exam earlier than the scheduled date so he could make the doctor's appointment. The professor agreed and gave Jerry the exam along with the blue book and told Jerry that when he was finished he was to put the blue book in his desk drawer and he would grade it when he graded all the others. Jerry wrote down all the questions on the test and put his name on the empty blue book and slipped this blue book in the professor's desk drawer while taking another blue book. Jerry then went to Lauinger Library with the blue book and the test questions and found all the correct answers, wrote them in the second blue book and then wrote his name on this blue book. The problem now was to switch these books without being noticed and before the professor has a chance to open the first blue book he previously put in his desk. Jerry's solution was to create a diversion of some sort in order to get to the professor's desk drawer to make the switch, so, he decided to set a waste basket on fire in the men's room activating the fire alarm and causing everyone to evacuate the building which would then allow him time to make the big switch of the blue books. Well, poor Jerry would never make a good "Torch" (arsonist) as the fire got out of control setting off the alarms and the sprinkler system and as our officers were clearing the building of personnel he was found inside the professor's office meddling with the desk drawer which was locked. You know the old adage of the best laid plans often go awry...this is a prime example. Jerry was arrested for arson and transported to the Second district then the case was turned over to the DC Fire Department. Fortunately, no one was injured, but, there was substantial damage to the men's room. Jerry had planned this for quite some time because he had stolen the doctor's letterhead stationary during a previous appointment with him and then he typed up the letter for the early exam himself and signed the doctor's name which constitutes forgery. Needless to say, Jerry was expelled from school in addition to facing criminal charges of arson and forgery. Isn't it amazing what lengths some people will go to just to avoid a little bit of studying.

One day I got a call from one of the female students complaining about being harassed by a former male student who was currently enrolled in Georgetown University Medical School. Gerald Cunningham was a problem while he was an undergraduate. During his senior year the 14" X 18" brass Darnall Hall sign that had been attached to Darnall Hall was stolen from the front of the building, but, had not been reported. By coincidence I had the occasion to be in Copley Hall where Cunningham lived and as I passed his room the door was wide open and what to my wondering eyes should appear? The Darnall Hall sign...sitting on top of his bureau just a big as life. Because of the "plain view" doctrine I knocked on his door and after he answered I identified myself and showed him my badge and told him that I was going to confiscate the sign as contraband of a theft. At that point I advised him of his Miranda rights (even though I hadn't placed him under arrest) and asked how he came into possession of the sign. He advised me that it was given to him by a friend, however, he refused to give up the name of this friend, so, I informed that he could be arrested for possession of stolen property and depending on the cost of the sign it could be a felony. While I was in the room I saw a small white envelope almost stuffed with fingernail clippings. I asked what they were for and he said that at the end of each semester he would send them to whatever professor he liked the least. He also told me that at Halloween he likes to go the cemeteries and howl at the moon, but, I merely took that as a joke and took possession of the sign and told him to be in my office at nine o'clock the following morning.

When Cunningham appeared in my office as directed I advised him of the cost of the sign which wasn't enough to warrant a felony charge, however, he was told that he was being brought before the Student Adjudication for possession of stolen property. After this case had been disposed of I'd had several minor complaints about Cunningham from other residents of Copley Hall about his weird actions, but, that was out of my jurisdiction and fell within the Resident Director's responsibility. After Cunningham graduated I had no more thoughts about him until I received this phone call. Ann Baker, the complainant, related to me that she and Cunningham had been dating for quite some time and recently they had gone to upstate New York. Ann told me that on their way back to D.C. an argument developed in the car and he pulled the car over to the side of the road, slapped her in the face a few times and then made her get out of the car and he drove away leaving her stranded on the highway. She said she was finally able to get a ride to the next town where she was able to get a bus back to her residence here in the District. Ever since that episode Cunningham has been calling her phone constantly and leaving messages for her to call him. Some of the messages fell just short of being threatening in nature, but, they were real enough for her to call my office. I provided her with the phone number of certain agencies to contact and advised her to get a restraining order against him. In the meantime I contacted Cunningham and told him that any further unlawful actions on his part could result in his arrest. His response was that he was a medical student now and I couldn't do anything to him. I told him that I also have jurisdiction in the Medical School and the Law School and he should watch himself. Inasmuch as I was on very good terms with the Dean of Medical School I made an appointment and discussed this matter with him. I told the Dean that I certainly wouldn't want anyone like Cunningham performing any surgery on me and recommended that he take this matter very seriously. He requested that I set up a meeting with him, Ann, and me. Two days later the meeting was held in his office and Ann told the Dean her story. She further stated other instances where Cunningham would lose his temper at the slightest provocation and would go into a rage and throw things around and beat on walls. I advised the Dean of my encounters with him as an undergraduate and suggested that Cunningham be removed from the School of Medicine. I also advised the Dean of my latest conversation with Cunningham. Two weeks later I received a formal notification that Mr. Cunningham had been expelled from Medical School and was no longer allowed to come onto this university property. Ann had also received a copy of the letter and when I spoke to her she advised me that she did have a restraining order against him in force. Looking back on that case I can't help wondering how many lives I might have saved by keeping this man out of reach of a scalpel.

On another occasion I had received a phone call from an FBI agent requesting a meeting to discuss a very important and urgent situation. I told him to come on out to my office and within the hour he was explaining to me the extortion case he was working on involving the Lauinger Library of the university. He stated that four different families in Fairfax County, Virginia had received letters stating that if they didn't place $25,000.00 in certain books in the Lauinger Library their daughters would have acid thrown in their faces on their wedding day. The perpetrator had stipulated a particular date and provided the titles and call numbers of the books that the money was to be placed in. These books had been checked out by the perpetrator and the insides had been hollowed out to where a packet of money could be inserted. He then returned the books back to their shelves. These particular books were located in four different sections of the library, so, it was necessary to set up four surveillance cameras to cover these shelves. We discussed this matter with Mr. Lamb who in turn contacted John Quinn, the head librarian, and asked him to come to our office. John came right away and was briefed on the situation and it was determined that he would have the library closed the following day under the pretense of having the air conditioning system repaired. This way the FBI agents could bring in their equipment, set up their surveillance cameras and establish an area for monitoring the cameras. During this operation there were only three people on the entire campus that knew anything about this other than me and that was Jeff Horton, Assistant Director; Mr. Lamb, Director; and Mr. Quinn, Librarian.

The FBI had provided the bait money and had the serial numbers on the money recorded and a homing device had been inserted in the brown paper wrapped packet placed inside each book. The stage was all set and the only thing now was to wait for the perpetrator to show up and check out these books. On the target date, which was a Saturday, I and Jeff Horton reported early to the office and joined the FBI agents in the waiting game. At about 1:30pm we got the word that a male person was at the book shelves removing these selected books from their shelves and he proceeded to the check out counter. The perpetrator was allowed to check out the books and leave the library and after he got about fifteen feet from the library FBI agents were all over him like ants on candy. The suspect was arrested without incident and immediately removed from the campus. The Agent in Charge thanked us for our help and advised that he would keep in touch. On the following Monday morning I received a call from him and he told us that the perpetrator was a PHD candidate at the University of Maryland and needed the money to pay for his education. He had gotten the names of the prospective victims from the wedding announcements in the society pages. To the best of my knowledge all these young ladies had their weddings without any drastic incidents and the perpetrator is now doing a lot of time in prison.

About a week later I was called into Mr. Lamb's office where he presented me with a letter of commendation signed by the Special Agent in Charge of the Washington Field Office of the FBI. Mr. Lamb also congratulated me told me to take the rest of the day off. I did!

In November or December of 1988 the campus organization of the Gay and Lesbian Association (GALA) was having a conference meeting at the posh and ritzy 1789 Restaurant located on the corner of 36th Street and Prospect Street. There was quite a bit of controversy about this organization which resulted in a protest demonstration by the American Nazi Party which had its headquarters on the other side of the Potomac River in Arlington, Virginia. Inasmuch as this was a university sanctioned event the campus police was detailed to monitor the situation and maintain peace in case the demonstration started to get out of hand. These members of the Nazi Party were all dressed in their Sunday best khaki uniforms with their swastika arm bands and their riot helmets with the face shields. They were carrying protest signs just like the labor pickets do. Prior to their arrival Jeff Horton and I placed ourselves in the most advantageous location where we could observe almost every action and be able to respond immediately. Upon the arrival of the Nazi's I radioed for one of our officers in the area to record the license numbers of the cars that they arrived in. Bill Auth, the university photographer was also present and I requested that he get as many pictures as possible of the Nazi demonstrators with the emphasis on their faces. The Nazi's weren't in position very long before they started to get taunted by our students. In a short time students of the Georgetown University Jewish Federation appeared bearing their own signs protesting the Nazi's and Adolph Hitler (even though old Adolph was dead and buried). This was when the situation started to get a little tenuous and it looked as though there might be the start of World War III. Some of the Jewish students got right up into the faces of the Nazi's and seemed to be begging for a confrontation, so, Jeff and I had to intervene to practically protect the Nazi's from annihilation. With all this activity we didn't have time to think about how cold it was until someone mentioned that I had better do something to cover my ears as they looked like they were about to fall off my head. Fortunately, the weather finally got to the Nazi's too along with the student protestors and they departed the scene, the students went back about their business and everything returned to normal. Jeff and I returned to our offices. A short time later I received a phone call from one of the students who had been at the scene and was told that one of the Nazi demonstrators was James Nugent, a student at Georgetown. I started doing some investigation and got his class schedule from the Registrar's Office and interviewed some of his instructor's and his classmates. Mr. Nugent, apparently, was not a very likeable person. According to many of his instructors he was very argumentative in class. Especially during the World History course which was being taught by Rabbi Harold White. Rabbi White advised me that there had been a couple incidents when Mr. Nugent got so fired up and angry in class that he stormed out of the classroom. Further investigation revealed that Mr. Nugent was also a member of the United States Marine Corps Reserve. Inasmuch as I had retired from the military service after twenty five years of active duty I knew that this was a violation of the Loyalty Oath one swears to when entering any branch of the military. Consequently, I contacted the Provost Marshal at the Henderson Hall Marine Base in Arlington and requested a meeting with him to discuss this matter. Prior to this meeting Bill Auth provided me with numerous photos of the demonstration and the participants. I made a copy of my investigation report and the following afternoon I proceeded to Henderson Hall and met with the Provost Marshal, Major Robert

Atkinson, at the Officer's Club where he treated me to lunch. After lunch we went to his office where I laid out the whole scenario and showed him the photos that were taken at the scene of Mr. Nugent in his Nazi uniform. I also provided him with a copy of my three page investigation report and told him not to hesitate to call me if I was ever needed as a witness. I returned to my office and discussed this case with my boss as to how it could best be handled on campus and as it turned out there was nothing we could do as Mr. Nugent hadn't violated any local statutes. Needless to say the status of this situation caused me quite a bit of consternation and I kept pondering different ways to get to Mr. Nugent legally when I got a visit from Rabbi White who informed me that Mr. Nugent had another fit of anger in his classroom to such a degree that he had to cancel the class. Nugent had called the Rabbi various names, made uncalled for ethnic slurs, and used extremely obscene and vulgar language. This was the straw that broke the camel's back and gave me the probable cause to handle Mr. Nugent. I had an officer dispatched to his room in the residence hall and brought to my office. Mr. Nugent was told in no uncertain terms exactly how I felt about the American Nazi Party and all the garbage they believed in. He just sat in his chair with a smirk on his face and his superior attitude. Then I told him to stand up and empty his pockets so I could pat him down for weapons pursuant to being arrested for disorderly conduct in a classroom (a little used law in the D.C. Criminal Code). Mr. Nugent was transported to Second District to be booked and then downtown to the Central Cell Block. While waiting for a trial date for Mr. Nugent I received a call from Major Atkinson advising that Nugent had received a courts martial and was dishonorably discharged from the Marine Corps Reserve. In view of these developments Mr. Lamb and I met with the Dean of Student Affairs and it was determined that Mr. Nugent would be expelled from the university for extreme unbecoming conduct and disruptive actions. I called Major Atkinson and advised him of our actions and he expressed his wholehearted approval. I hate being smirked at.

Not all of our cases dealt with thieves, burglars, and other elements of the criminal world. Such was the day when shortly after reporting for work I was informed that at approximately 7:30am there had been a male person who had dropped dead while jogging around the newly built athletic field. There was no identification on the person and he had already been removed to the Medical Examiner's office downtown. Inasmuch as this athletic field is used by off campus personnel also, it was unknown if he was a student or citizen of the local area.

I contacted the Medical Examiner and identified my self and requested that they take some Polaroid pictures of the person so I could have something to use in an attempt to make identification. After going to the ME's office and retrieving the photos (the ME was kind of enough to make a few copies) I gave some to our uniformed officers too. I contacted the Missing Persons section of Metropolitan Police Department to determine if there had been any reports of a male person matching the description of our decedent. No report had been filed. I canvassed the campus showing the picture to numerous students, faculty, and staff members. After about three hours one of the students said he looked familiar and could I show it to another student for confirmation. Bingo! Just before noon I had identified the person as David Grange, one of our students. I then proceeded to the Registrar's office to obtain all the information I could concerning this person. I was told that he was the nephew of Fred Parker, the Director of Financial Aid. Consequently, I had the undesirable task of telling Fred about his nephew. Fred was completely surprised because David appeared to be in the best of health. Fred also advised me that David's parents were out of the country and volunteered to accompany me downtown to make a positive identification. I made arrangements for transportation and Father Peter O'Shea also went with us for spiritual and moral support. Inasmuch as every death in the District (regardless of the cause) is investigated by the Homicide Division, the ME's office had already notified them and upon our arrival Detective Bill Wood was at the morgue. I had worked with Bill on a couple other fatalities involving the university and he was a top notch homicide detective.

After the positive identification was completed Fred made the arrangements for having Dave taken to a funeral home. Fred also stated that he would make the necessary notifications to his brother and sister-in-law. Bill Wood and I offered Fred our deepest condolences and whatever assistance we might be able to provide. A few days later we were informed by the ME that the cause of death was an enlarged heart. Such a shame that someone so young had to be taken away even before he reached the prime of his life.

As I mentioned I had worked with Bill Wood on other fatalities. We first met while the Concentrated Care Center, an addition to the hospital was being built. At about 3:30pm one spring day I was notified of an accident at that construction site and that the injured person had been taken to the emergency room and a detective from the Homicide Division was enroute to that location. I responded there and within minutes Bill Wood arrived and we introduced ourselves. After fifteen minutes in the emergency room the injured person expired from multiple fractures, broken bones, and internal hemorrhaging. Once we had obtained all the necessary information and personal data of the victim we proceeded to the accident site and interviewed what witnesses there were. The victim was on a scaffold about the equivalent of three stories high and was inspecting some overhead work that had just been completed. While concentrating on the overhead work area he walked right off the end of the scaffold which had no safety bar or strap attached to it as required by law. Both Bill and I were surprised that the victim lived as long as he did after a fall of that distance. After gathering the information pertaining to the accident we returned to the emergency room where the victim's wife was waiting. She was extremely shaken and crying her eyes out. Bill took her into his arms to console her and tried to make her as comfortable as he could under very trying circumstances. Seeing the way Bill handled the victim's wife told me that he was a very compassionate person with a heart as big as all outdoors. Bill was able to make contact with a friend of the wife and we both waited with her until that person came to help care for her and take her home. It's not surprising that a few years later while I was reading a Reader's Digest magazine that I ran across a feature story about Bill Wood, Homicide Detective.

Another interesting case was in April of 1987. Juan Diaz, a student living off campus stepped out on his front porch on Easter Sunday to get the morning newspaper and discovered a cardboard box on the porch. The box was not there the night before, so, out of curiosity, Juan opened it up to see what was inside. Juan couldn't believe his eyes and was stunned when he saw a human head inside the box. He left the box where it was and immediately called the police. Our office was notified inasmuch as a Georgetown University student was involved and I was called at home to come in on the case. I arrived at Juan's house and met with my old friend Kevin McCarthy of 2-D. We got what information we could from Juan and then had the box and its contents taken to the MPD Forensics Laboratory. I had to call in two more investigator's as we had to go to the medical school anatomy department and inventory every cadaver in an effort to determine if the head came from there. All the body parts were accounted for and there was no missing head. Naturally, Homicide Division was called into the case also and who should appear...none other than Bill Wood. Bill, jokingly, said that we would have to quit meeting like this and all three of us laughed a little. This was a really grim task trying to locate someone who might know who the person was that once had this head on their neck. We even resorted to the Washington Post by having a picture of the head appear in the paper along with a brief explanation. We still didn't have any luck and the case was getting very cold and after three weeks with no leads or additional information we put the case in a suspended status until further information became available. Here it is now 2005 and to the best of my knowledge, as of this writing, the origin of this head has not yet been determined.

There was a lot of construction being done on campus during the 1980's and on one particular occasion, early in the morning, a construction worker called our department to report a stranger sleeping on the third level of what was to become one of the apartment buildings of Village "B". I had just arrived at my office and didn't give it a second thought as our uniformed officers would take care of the situation. Just as I had made myself a cup of coffee and started to review the reports of the previous day the dispatcher called me and said that there might be a dead man at the construction site. I left my office and proceeded to that location to investigate the matter and sure enough, the over night guest was dead. Second District was notified who in turn notified the Homicide Division.

The area was cordoned off and I, along with one of my other investigator's secured the area and waited for the members of the Metropolitan Police to arrive. The month was May and the weather had been quite pleasant, so, the person didn't appear to have died from exposure, however, at the scene there were two empty whiskey bottles and the corpse reeked of alcohol. In the absence of an autopsy it would seem that the person had drunk himself to death. He bore no identification, so, I thought here we go again with another "John Doe" case. Fortunately, one of the uniformed officer's of Second District recognized the corpse as one of the homeless persons that usually hung around the bottom of Wisconsin Avenue near the Potomac River. The officer stated that he'd had a run in with the decedent a couple of times for panhandling.

It seems strange that every time two or three police cars are at a particular location, people appear out of the woodwork to see what was going on. I guess it is human nature to be curious. The corpse was removed from the site and everything returned to normal and I finally got a chance to drink my cold coffee.

In 1976 while the United States was celebrating its bicentennial, Reverend (and I use the title very precariously) Sun Myung Moon decided that he too would get some of the action. Inasmuch as he has conducted such mass weddings he figured he would have a mass rally on July 4, 1976 in Washington, DC. Consequently he had thousands of his followers (known as Moonies) spread out all over the United States and centering their efforts on college campuses. On the face of things they were merely supposed to be handing out flyers inviting everyone to the rally which was going to be in the Redskins Football stadium. Twenty-five of them appeared on our campus and went to the receptionist of Healy Building and very politely asked if they could leave their box lunches there for about fifteen minutes. The receptionist didn't see any harm in that for fifteen minutes, so, she agreed. They left their lunches and then went to work on the campus. After two hours the lunches were still there and the receptionist called my office inquiring what to do. I proceeded to her office and got what information she had concerning these people and provided me with one of their flyers. As soon as I saw these people were affiliated with the Unification Church I knew we were in for a lot of trouble. I had Charlie Adkins and Jim McNally, two of my investigators, meet me and we took all the box lunches and threw them in the nearest dumpster. Then I assigned Charlie Adkins to the receptionist office in the event they returned for their lunches. Jim and I then scoured the campus looking for these individuals. I finally located the leader of the group and after I identified myself and showed him my badge I told him he had fifteen minutes to gather every one of his people and get off campus. At this the leader started to argue with me as to their right to be there in a public place. This guy was beginning to get under my skin, so, I unloaded on him and told him that this was private property and I had full arrest powers and if he uttered one more word he would be arrested for Unlawful Entry. He asked me about the lunches and I told him we ate them and what was left over we gave to our sentry dogs (actually we don't have any sentry dogs, but, they didn't need to know that). Naturally there was much grumbling going on and a lot of nasty looks being cast in our direction, but, they were escorted off campus and each one was given a written warning about violating certain portions of the D. C. Criminal Code. The very next morning as I arrived at work I saw a large assemblage in front of the Healy Gates. Once I got to my office I was told that there were a lot of Moonies at the gate protesting about not being allowed on campus. My boss and I met with the Provost and I gave him the background information about the Unification Church and how they recruit kids from high schools and college campuses. I further advised the Provost that I had done some extensive research of the Unification Church and other cults as well and convinced him that they were bad news and could be extremely hazardous to have on campus. We assigned two uniformed officers to monitor the situation and persuaded the students to ignore the protestors and go on about their business. After about three hours, the Moonies saw their action was not getting them anywhere, so, they departed the area, and two days later I was called to the Presidents Office in response to a letter that he had received from an organization named the Alliance for the Preservation of Religious Liberties (APRL). According to them I was an anti Christ devil that deprived the rights of Christians to assemble and prosthletize the Unification Church. I had all my research material with me and after a rather lengthy discussion and providing sufficient evidence to support my actions it was decided that a letter would be sent to APRL explaining the universities position on religious cults. In short, the letter sent from the President' office boiled down to telling them to go pound sand. Unfortunately, it seemed to be a case of "a day late and a dollar short", because, as it turned out later on the Moonies had already gotten their foot in the door. About two months after that incident as I was walking down the hallway in Healy basement I saw a strange looking poster on one of the bulletin boards. It referred to an information meeting and get together in one of the classrooms in Loyola Hall in East Campus. This program was given by the Collegiate Association for the Research of Principles (CARP). For the uninformed, CARP is the primary recruiting group for the Unification Church. I took the poster down and proceeded to the office of the Dean of Academic Affairs who has the responsibility of assigning classrooms for various functions. One of the criteria to get a classroom is the request must be from a recognized campus organization such as the Jewish Student Alliance, or Georgetown Debate Society. My concern was who requested this classroom for this organization and I was given the name of James Fisher. I checked the student listing in the computer; however, this name never appeared. In the event it might be a late addition I went to the Registrar's Office and had them check their records for James Fisher and nothing appeared there either. I discussed this matter with Mr. Lamb and he agreed with my suggestion that I keep an eye on what transpires at this meeting. Because I was well known to the Moonies I assigned my investigator, Tony Marten to attend this meeting and report what all takes place. After reading Tony's report it turned out just as I suspected...they were trying to establish themselves further on this campus for the purpose of recruiting. High schools and college campuses are prime hunting grounds for recruiters of religious cults and they prey mostly on the freshmen students. For most of the freshmen students it's their first time away from home for a long period of time and more susceptible to the recruiter's methods. They "love bomb" you to tears. They make you feel that you're the greatest person on earth and the sun rises and sets on you. They invite you, individually, to their house for dinner and fun and games and make you feel completely relaxed in their company. After a week or so they invite you to a spiritual weekend retreat in fairly close campsite. And if you agree and go that retreat a week or so later they invite you to three or four day retreat at a location that is quite a bit farther away. After attending that little soiree you are now invited to a two week seminar which is normally held a couple of states away. There is never any expense paid out of your pocket…it's all free, but, by the end of the two week stay they have you and the indoctrination really gets serious until you actually believe that Reverend Sun Myung Moon is the true Messiah and you end up being a slave for him. I talked to Mr. Lamb about this situation and suggested that we let them have a couple more of their meetings; however, I would attend these other meetings along with Tony. After these meetings I felt we had enough evidence plus I spoke with one of the students who had been to the weekend retreat and was now invited for a five day retreat. This student provided me with a signed; five page statement detailing the events of her weekend retreat which smacked of their brainwashing techniques. I contacted Mr. Fisher at the next scheduled meeting and told the attendees that there would not be any more of these meetings and to say goodbye to Mr. Fisher. Tony and I escorted Mr. Fisher to my office where I told him I knew who he was and what his intentions were. I read him the riot act and advised him that he was *persona non gratis* (not welcomed) at this institution and all the other universities in the consortium is being notified of his activities. He was further advised that should he attempt to come on this campus again he would be arrested. Needless to say, the President's office received another letter from APRL accusing me again of being an antichrist and servant of the devil. This time the President's office didn't even bother with wasting paper to respond to them.

Not too long after that episode another poster appeared on the bulletin boards. This time it was the Divine Light Mission who had somehow managed to reserve a classroom for their assembly, but, before their scheduled meeting I met with the Dean's office and told them about this organization and they agreed to cancel the meeting. I suggested that in the future prior to giving out these classrooms they might want to check with my office as I had a complete listing of the various religious cults that were active in the District of Columbia area.

It was during this time when a couple of male students came to my office complaining about some guy's from the Church of Scientology hounding them for money. I listened to their stories and made a report of the complaints and inasmuch as students were involved I had probable cause to investigate the matter. I discussed with Mr. Lamb what my plan of action was and he agreed. Two days later in the evening hours I went to the location of the Founding Church of Scientology on 20th Street in the District. I was dressed in casual clothes and acted as though I didn't know anything about scientology. As a matter of fact I acted more like a Mr. Milquetoast. Upon my arrival I was greeted by a very attractive young lady who led me to a waiting area and told me someone would be with me shortly. While I was waiting I noticed that a male instructor would be assigned to a female and a female instructor would be assigned to a male. After several minutes of waiting I was conducted to a room where they had two empty coffee cans attached with a long string between. I was told to close my eyes and hold one can between my knees and the other can was held by my instructor. This went on for ten minutes and the instructor asked me if I had felt any electrical impulses to which I replied no. Well, she got a face on her and told me that I was in real need of enlightenment and professional guidance. Then I was given this 250 questionnaire to fill out and return to the front desk. This questionnaire asked all kinds of nutty things that made absolutely no sense at all. Upon completing this questionnaire and returning it to the front desk I sat and waited again. After about fifteen minutes I was taken to another part of the building and was handed over to an auditor who just happened to be another female. This auditor told me that I was rated very high in certain areas, but, there were a lot of other areas that needed immediate attention... namely communicating with people and having a good rapport. At that point I had to bite my cheek to keep from laughing because I was known for having a very good rapport, particularly with the students. After this auditing I was then escorted to the front desk where another nice looking young lady was waiting to sign me up for various recommended courses. Each course cost between $250.00 and $350.00 and had to be taken in the building I was in. I told the lady that I didn't have that kind of money on me and at that point she opened a desk drawer filled with blank checks from every bank in the area. I told her I couldn't write a check without my wife's approval or she would kill me and then I noticed two big, husky men approaching us so I started to act as though I was having a heart attack and told them that I needed some fresh air. They got me outside and after a few minutes I was left alone and proceeded on to my car and went home. This whole process must have taken about two hours and to be honest with you, I couldn't get out of that building fast enough. The next morning I told to Mr. Lamb about my experience and we both laughed about. With what they charge for their various courses you have to be wealthy like John Travolta to be a Scientologist as he is. And I kept wondering what all that business with the coffee cans was anyway? Those Scientologists are far out people, right along with L. Ron Hubbard, the founder of The Church of Scientology. And that is another question I never could figure out...why do they call it a church? I guess for tax purposes. Heck, if witches covens can get tax exempt status I guess L. Ron Hubbard figured he's entitled to it too.

For the longest time we'd had problems with the Moonies trying to recruit some of our students. One freshman complained to my office that he was being harassed all the time by some young guy's and girls who keep inviting him to their house in Georgetown for dinner and companionship. He had gone there once before, but, he had bad feelings about them so he never went back and they've been after him ever since to return. The student told me that they had even gone to his room in Xavier Hall and knocked on his door. Well, with this information we were in a different ball game, because now they were entering private property without invitation which constitutes unlawful entry…a misdemeanor in the District of Columbia. A couple of days later the student called me and advised me that he had gotten a phone call from them saying that they had a gift for him and was going to come by his room and drop it off that evening. I assigned Charlie Adkins and Jim McNally to assist me that evening and we positioned ourselves in Xavier Hall where we could keep the door to the student's room in view. At about 6:30pm two young men and a young girl appeared at the door and knocked three or four times and as the student opened his door we approached the subjects, identified ourselves and told them they were under arrest for unlawful entry. As I was putting the handcuffs on my guy he decided he didn't want to get locked up and started to run from the scene. I caught him after a short chase and slammed him up against the wall with his face to the wall. He continued to struggle, so, I placed my right knee very firmly in his back, and he started to sag to the floor when Charlie arrived and gave assistance. They were then transported to my office where we made out Field Contact Cards on them and took their pictures. Two units from MPD responded to transport them to Second District for booking and then transferred downtown to the Central Cell Block. Early the next morning I was at Superior Court to paper the case with the U. S. Attorney's Office. After this incident we had no more problems with the Moonies and their recruitment attempts. It felt right good getting my adrenalin flowing that night. Every once in a while you have to get a little action going so you don't atrophy and besides, what's the point of knowing the martial arts if you can't exercise that knowledge now and again?

One Monday morning as I was going over the reports of the previous weekend I heard a loud commotion in the dispatcher's area and went to see who was doing all the yelling and cussing. I saw this foreign looking man in a blue three piece suit acting in a very bazaar manner, so, I used as much tact and diplomacy as possible to get him to calm down long enough for me to find what his complaint was. As it turned out, the previous night he was parked, all alone, in an off limits area near the construction site of the new football field. Our Officer's saw him parked there and asked for his identity and for him to dismount from his vehicle. When asked why he was there he became very indignant with the officer's and started yelling at them in a foreign language. He was told to get in his car and leave the area to which he objected very strenuously, but, eventually complied.

I didn't see what the big deal was until he complained about getting some mud on his shoes and trousers when he got out of the car in the construction area. This guy, an Egyptian named Hamdi Sallah just wouldn't calm down and declared that he had diplomatic immunity and that he was a high ranking person with the Egyptian Embassy. After much cajoling and few "yes sir" and "no sir" I was finally able to get him to leave the building and I told him I would look into the matter. That is exactly what I did and to this day Mr. Sallah regrets he ever put on such a show. I contacted the Egyptian embassy and learned that Mr. Sallah was, at one time, the second secretary to the ambassador of Egypt, however, he had been relieved from that job eight months previously. I then contacted the State Department and gave them the Diplomatic Tag number on Sallah's car and his name. An hour later I received a call from a lady, Sally Franklin, at the State Department who advised me that particular tag number had been revoked for two years and should we see the tag again we were to confiscate it. Our Registrar's Office showed that Mr. Sallah was listed as a part time student, however, he hadn't attended any classes for three months and was dropped from the rolls, plus, he had an outstanding balance of $250.00 for overdue books at the Lauinger Library. The University Traffic Office had a bunch of parking tickets against Sallah's car totaling $465.00. Armed with this information I could hardly wait for Mr. Sallah's return to see what action I had taken against our officer's. One day the following week at about 9:00am Mr. Sallah appeared at the O'Gara Building all dressed up in his three piece suit. I invited him into my office and gave him a seat. After he was seated I had one of our officer's come into the office and I instructed him to go to Mr. Sallah's car and remove the DPL tags. I thought Sallah was going to have a fit as he jumped up out of the chair, but, I stopped him from leaving my office and then he started yelling at me. I told him to shut his mouth and listen or I'd lock him up and turn him over to the State Department. Then I unloaded on him all the information that I had gathered about him advising him that he did not, nor did he ever have diplomatic immunity and that he owed the University $715.00 in overdue book fines and parking violations. I told him he had 72 hours to pay this debt or a warrant would be issued for his arrest. I also had the Traffic Department tow his car to the impound lot. Immediately after he left my office I called Ms. Franklin, who had been so helpful at the State Department and told her what had happened. She requested, and received, a copy of my four page chronological investigative report so she could take follow up action from her office. One week later I received a call from Ms. Franklin thanking me for the return of the DPL tags that Sallah had been using and she also advised me that based on the information I had provided her, Mr. Sallah had been deported back to Egypt. The Egyptian embassy had sent a letter of apology for Sallah's actions along with a certified check in the amount of $715.00. To my satisfaction everything turned out real good. I often wonder if Hamdi Sallah ever got over his self importance. He had an ego as big as the Yankee Stadium.

Another deportation case that I was involved with concerned one of our students from the Ivory Coast who was living in Alban Towers, a high rise apartment building on Wisconsin Avenue the University owned. Dwan Umballah, the student involved, had written several checks to Georgetown University totaling well over $3,000 and they all bounced due to insufficient funds. I went to his apartment in Alban Towers to discuss the matter with him, however, his knowledge of the English language was very limited, and he ended up calling some attorney downtown that was from his country. I met with the attorney, Mr. Said Omni, that same afternoon and it was determined that he would contact the student's father in the Ivory Coast and have the money wired to America. I tacitly agreed to this pending approval of the Bursars Office. Two days later Mr. Omni appeared at my office with over $3,000 in American currency to satisfy the overdrafts. We proceeded to the office of Accounts Payable and settled the matter. Mr. Omni instructed Dwan not to write anymore checks and gave me his office and home phone numbers if there were any more problems with Dwan. Mr. Omni had apparently been appointed by Dwan's father to be his guardian while he was in this country. Dwan came from a very wealthy family, but, felt that he could do whatever he wanted and his father would clean up whatever mess may result from his actions. At first I thought that it might be a lack of communication with Dwan, but, I later found out, accidentally, that he actually could speak English quite well. After a while it seemed that I was calling Mr. Omni several times a week concerning Dwan's activities. He had, on a few occasions, been disruptive in class and at one point was told to leave the class by the instructor. He had been involved with starting a few fights on campus at various locations, Once in the Center Pub, another time in Healy Basement and a couple of times on Healy Lawn. The straw that broke the camels back was when he tried to force himself on a female student who didn't want anything to do with him. I contacted Mr. Omni and advised him that Dwan's actions could no longer be tolerated and that I was going initiate action to have him removed from the University and its property, including Alban Towers. Mr. Omni and I had enjoyed an amiable relationship, but, Dwan's actions were creating a very strong strain on this relationship. Fortunately, the girl had not been harmed, but, Dwan had put such a scare in her that she was given round-the-clock protection from him. It finally got to the point where Dwan wouldn't follow the instructions of Mr. Omni, so, I advised Mr. Omni that I was going to do what I could to have Dwan sent back to the Ivory Coast. I contacted my friend at the State Department and requested information on deporting an individual to the Ivory Coast. She faxed me all the material I needed and within two days Dwan was on his way back home. Needless to say, Dwan didn't like me very well and said that one day I will be very sorry for what I am doing to him...that was back in 1987 and to this day I still don't have any qualms about my actions. Mr. Omni even called me and thanked me for what I did because he told me Dwan was like an albatross around his neck. At least three people were satisfied with the results, me, Mr. Omni, and the scared female student (who wasn't scared anymore).

I doubt very seriously if there is any learning institution that is without some type of a drug problem. I know that Georgetown University wasn't immune from the drug problem either. One such case involved a student named Zack Connery who was in his junior year and majored in mathematics and Chinese. Zack resided in Loyola Hall on the East Campus and had a thriving business...selling drugs. I'd had some information from an informant about the drug trafficking, but, the informant couldn't name who was involved and what was being sold. Tony Marten was my youngest looking investigator, so, we made arrangements and a cover story for him to attend classes and mingle in with the other students. Tony worked undercover for almost two months reporting daily to me by phone. One evening as I was about to sit down for dinner at my home I got a call from Tony advising that Zack had gotten a rather large supply of drugs that afternoon and that he was going to be making his distribution that same evening. I advised Tony to make a purchase of whatever he could. I contacted Mr. Lamb at his home and advised him as to what was taking place and he stated that he would meet me at the office. At 7:00pm we met at my office and Mr. Lamb asked where I wanted him to be as it was my operation and I was in charge. I posted Mr. Lamb on the street below the window of Zack's room in the event he might toss some of the drugs out the window as there wasn't a toilet in his room to flush it down the drain. At 7:30pm armed with a search warrant I and Jeff Horton along with the watch commander, Sgt. Eugene Nock and three other uniformed officers proceeded to the third floor of Loyola Hall. Upon our arrival on the floor there were several students in the hallway outside Zack's room and as one of them was about to give a warning to Zach of our presence I clamped my hand over his mouth and told him, very quietly, to shut his mouth or he would be arrested for aiding and abetting. Fortunately the door was not locked, so all we had to do was turn the knob and enter. Upon entry into the room I advised everyone to stay right where they were and once we were all in the room I posted an officer outside the door. Zach was in the process of cutting and packaging a white powdery substance (later tested positive as cocaine) and already packaged several bindles of the stuff. These bindles were marked with Chinese writing to identify who they were to be delivered to. We confiscated all of his paraphernalia, drugs, money, and even a ledger book where he maintained all of his drug transactions. Zach was arrested along with all the other persons that were in the room and read their Miranda rights. They were then transported to our offices where they were interrogated and provided written statements as to their involvement with Zack's operation. The ledger we confiscated was a gold mine of information as it contained the names of his clients, their drug of choice, the amount, and cost of each transaction, and the dates and quantities of various drugs he received. I will have to admit that Zach was very cooperative while he was in my office, but, the students that worked for him became a little mouthy, so, I had to straighten them out and let them know that they were in deep trouble and the more they ran their mouths the harder it was going to be for them. I then told them about spending the night at the Central Cell block and that shut them up in a heart beat. Second District narcotics detectives were notified and responded to our offices where we ran field tests on the various drugs we confiscated. Strangely enough, when we ran tests on the hashish they kept showing up negative. We must have run about five or six field tests and they all came up negative. I asked Zack what that substance was and he advised that it was hashish. When he was told the tests were showing negative he started getting extremely nervous. A few days later after we got the report from the Drug Enforcement Agency (DEA) I could understand why. What Zach was selling as hashish turned out to be compressed cow manure. With this information I questioned Zach again as to who his sources were, but, he refused to give any names, so I told him I was going to tell everyone he sold the "hashish" to what it really was and let them take care of business of getting their money back from him or face the alternative. Consequently, Zach decided that it would be in his best interest to roll over and he provided the names of his suppliers and this information was passed on to the Second District detectives.

During a meeting in the office of the Dean of Student Affairs, Zach was there with his attorney and his mother and father, Mr. Lamb, Jeff Horton, and me. The purpose of this meeting was for Zack's parents to plead that he not be expelled from school and the University to drop the charges against him in criminal court. I couldn't believe my ears and mentioned to them about the female student that he had gotten hooked on drugs and ended up withdrawing from school because of her addiction. At this point Mrs. Connery started crying and asked me if I had no sympathy for her son. I flatly told her "Madam, if you are looking for sympathy it's between s**t and syphilis in the dictionary"! Needless to say, there was quite a flurry in the room after that and both Jeff and Mr. Lamb were laughing and the dean had a smile on his face. Zack, his parents and his attorney all left the room in a huff and then the dean started to laugh also. Zack got expelled.

A few months later during his trial while I was on the witness stand Zack's attorney was doing his best to get me to name my informants and the name of my undercover investigator and I adamantly refused to disclose that information. This frustrated Zack's attorney so much that he attempted to discredit me on the stand and in doing so he got the wrath of the judge and was told "...this is not a capital offense case and you are certainly not Perry Mason, so, stop hounding this witness as he doesn't have to disclose that information". Embarrassed, the attorney didn't ask anymore questions and I stepped down from the witness stand. Zack was found guilty on all charges and specifications and at the sentencing phase he received fifteen years in prison with ten years being suspended.

Another informant, whom I'd had a stand off with previously, came to my office and advised me that he had a lot of information on a lot of different drug dealers both on and off the campus. I immediately called the narcotics detectives at Second District as this was going to be a joint investigation. Lieutenant John Sarney and detectives Jerry Wright, and Nick Demiduck came to my office and listened to the information that my informant had to give them. This meeting lasted almost two hours and when the detectives left they couldn't thank me enough for the information they had gotten.

This investigation lasted for about two and a half months with the 2D detectives making numerous buys both on and off the campus. One warm spring evening while I was at home Lt. Sarney called me and advised me that they had eighteen arrest warrants and suggested that I come back to the campus. I contacted Mr. Lamb to let him know what was happening and he stated that he would meet me at the office too. I arrived at my office and called Lt. Sarney to let him now I was there and that Mr. Lamb was going to join us. Twenty minutes later Lt. Sarney, Jerry, Nick, Mr. Lamb and I was discussing the manner the arrest were going to take place. I would accompany the detectives when they made the arrests on campus as Mr. Lamb made the necessary notifications to the various university officials. Eleven students were arrested that night on campus and the rest lived off campus. Not all the arrestees were students, but, some of them were former or graduated students. We worked well into the early morning hours and after the arrests we still had to go downtown to paper the cases in Superior Court. It wasn't until early afternoon that I got finished at the court house and returned to the campus. Mr. Lamb was so pleased with the way things had transpired that he gave me the next two days off to relax and catch up on my sleep. This had been a very demanding investigation, but, the results were outstanding. Needless to say all the students involved not only had to stand trial in town, they also had to be brought before the Student Adjudication Board where they were found guilty and suspended from school. Inasmuch as there were two different jurisdictions involved there was no violation of the double jeopardy statute. None of them ever did come back to school.

Suicide is an ugly way to solve personal problems and very devastating on the friends and next of kin of the person committing such an act. Unfortunately, there were a few that occurred at Georgetown University that I had to investigate along with detectives of the MPD Homicide Division. The first such case happened one spring day at about 3:45pm. A male student from American University had been involved in a romantic relationship that had gone sour and came to Georgetown to talk to and commiserate with one of his friends who was one of our students. Unable to find his friend he managed to gain access to the roof of Reiss Science Building where he decided to leave this world by doing a header from the roof. This building is a six story structure with an overhead cover at the entrance to the building and this is where the victim landed rather than on the cement sidewalk after his departure from the roof. During the initial phase of the investigation I proceeded to the point of departure to see if there was a note or any personal effects the victim may have left behind. As I was up on the roof I looked down to where the victim the paramedics were still working on the victim and it was at that time when I suddenly got this fear of heights. As a former paratrooper in the Army, heights never bothered me at all as could be evidenced while I was investigating the loss of the clock hands when I had to crawl along the slate roofs of the Jesuit Community and climb around on the cross beams in the lofts of Healy Building. The cause of death was evident, however, without witnesses it could not be classified as a suicide, accident, or a homicide. The next phase of the investigation was to locate a witness which encompassed interviewing hundreds of people who might have seen what took place. I had my other investigators and uniformed officers canvas the area of Reiss Science Building. At about 6:30pm as I was interviewing students living in Copley Hall I found a female student whose room window faces Reiss Science Building and she related to me that while she was watering her plant that hung at that window she saw the victim jump from the building. When I asked her why didn't she report it she said she had fainted and when she regained consciousness she remained dizzy, incoherent and could not believe what she had seen. I made contact with one of the homicide detectives who met with me and I introduced him to the witness who repeated her story to him as to what she had witnessed. I was able to get her personal data and a written statement from her and gave it to the homicide detectives after making a copy for my files. The Investigator at American University, John Walsh, was notified as soon as we discovered the victim was one of their students and he investigated the matter at their campus and provided me with the necessary background information leading up to this tragic incident. John provided me with a copy of his investigative report and I in turn submitted a copy to the homicide detectives. All the bases seemed to be covered and with the witnesses statement the case could now be ruled as a suicide. I don't know what it was about the Reiss Science Building, but, a couple of years later there was another suicide that occurred there on the third floor in a science laboratory. This time there was no doubt that it was suicide because the victim left a seven page letter explaining why he took his life. At first glance it was thought to be an overdose as his method of dying was the use of laughing gas (nitrous oxide). However, the contents of his letter substantiated the classification of suicide. There was not much to investigate in this incident as it was all written out in his letter and not to make light of the situation, but, at least he went out laughing. That's better than a lot of us do.

One time in the fall of 1988 we had a student from France who was diagnosed as extremely disturbed and borderline suicidal, but, he refused to be hospitalized and according to the law in the District of Columbia a person cannot be institutionalized unless a doctor determines that he is a threat to himself or to others. None of his doctors wanted to make such a determination, so, he was confined to his residence hall room on the third floor of Darnall Hall with a uniformed officer posted outside his door until we could get a doctor to commit him. This procedure lasted for two days with a uniformed officer at his door twenty four hours a day. The student did have to leave his room periodically to use the bathroom and to take a shower and each time an officer had to escort him to and from the bathroom. On the third night on one such occasion as they were on their way to the bathroom the student suddenly turned around, knocked the officer out of the way and ran out the door going out onto the patio area. Once outside he then climbed over the four foot high wall surrounding the patio area and jumped to the ground. Our officers called for an ambulance and rushed to where he was lying and administered first aid. In minutes the ambulance arrived and transported the student to the

Georgetown University Hospital emergency room which was only about three hundred yards away. The doctors worked on him for several hours as he had broken both legs, one arm and sustained numerous injuries to the rest of his body and head. Naturally, our officer was unrightfully blamed for lack of caution, but, this was an uncontrollable situation and the officer was caught completely by surprise. Consequently, at about 1:30 in the morning I was called in from home and took control of the investigation. After gathering all the information available and interviewing the doctors that were involved I concluded that the fault for this tragedy laid squarely on the shoulders of the doctors who initially diagnosed the student as disturbed and borderline suicidal and those doctors who refused to have him committed. As for the student bolting from our officer as he did, that could have happened to anyone of us, so, I saw no fault on the part of the officer. It was unfortunate that the student didn't survive all of his injuries, but it must be stressed that our department did everything possible to prevent this from happening.

On another occasion, one sunny weekday afternoon, a female student from France was standing on the parapet on the outer side of the wall on Darnall Hall patio. Almost the same spot where the previous student had jumped from. I was in my office at the time when I got the call and responded to the scene. I met with the Resident Director (RD) and the girls Resident Assistant (RA) and obtained what information they had about the girl. Her name was Lynette Laroux and she was from Paris. Her roommate advised that Lynette was extremely homesick and depressed about her school work and academic load. No one else was on the patio and I eased my way out the door and proceeded to the opposite wall away from where Lynette was standing. I just meandered about for a few minutes so as not to startle her and to let her know that someone else was on the patio. As I turned around I acted surprised to see her and said "Hi". Surprisingly she responded and I engaged myself with some small talk about the weather and school and classes I was taking at George Mason University. All the time I was talking to her I kept edging myself a little closer to her bit by bit. During this time I was as nervous as a cat in a room full of rocking chairs and kept praying silently to be able to reach her before she did something drastic. After about twenty minutes I was able to get within an arms length from Lynette and was able to ask her questions about herself and as she was responding I instantly reached out with my left hand and grabbed her left wrist and put my other arm around her waist and was able to get her over the wall and onto the patio to safety. The RD and the RA rushed to where we were and took control of Lynette and took her to a doctor. All of a sudden I was drenched in sweat and couldn't stop shaking from nerves. I think the only other time I was as scared as that was when we were caught in crossfire in the Korean War. I kept thinking what if I said something wrong or made a move that might frighten her into doing something bad. God, if I never have to do anything like that again it will be too soon and I thanked the Lord for giving me the ability to do what I did. The Resident Director and the Resident Assistant sent letters of appreciation to my boss and the Dean of Student Affairs also sent a letter of congratulations on a job well done to my boss. About two weeks later Lynette came to my office to apologize for her actions and to thank me for what I had done and she told me how she was doing and how her treatments were going. I told her no thanks were necessary as I was just doing my job. Just before she left my office she kissed me on the cheeks and thanked me again and left. I felt good all over. There is nothing like a happy ending.

Among the law enforcement community of colleges and universities there is an organization named the International Association of Campus Law Enforcement Administrators (IACLEA). IACLEA was formulated back in November 1958 when the security directors of eleven colleges and universities met on the campus of Arizona State University to discuss job challenges and mutual problems and possible solutions for these problems. Today this organization represents over 1,000 colleges and universities and acts as a clearing house for information and issues shared by campus security directors across the country. This organization is broken down into various regions and each region has certain higher learning institutions within their consortium. Georgetown University is a member of the Mid Atlantic Region and every month this consortium has business meetings at one of the schools in the group. There is an annual conference which is hosted by one of the member institutions which contains a professional program and informal participation aimed toward discussions of mutual problems, needs, and solutions to these problems. This is a very productive organization and it also publishes, bimonthly, the Campus Law Enforcement Journal which is loaded with good information for all members of the campus law enforcement community.

Based on the mission statement and structure of IACLEA, I thought it would be a good idea if all the investigators of the schools in our consortium could meet on a monthly basis to discuss our mutual problems, exchange information on possible suspects, and establish some form of organization. Consequently, in 1985 I mailed letters to all the investigators of our consortium outlining my suggestion and requested their input. My idea was readily accepted by all of the investigators and the following week we held our first meeting at Georgetown University where I laid out my proposal to establish the Campus Police Investigators Association. Everyone agreed on the proposal and work was started right then to develop the bi-laws and constitution of the organization. In its infancy there were seven schools involved; Georgetown University, George Washington University, American University, Howard University, Gaulladet University, University of D.C., and the Catholic University of America. In the interim of our next meeting there were small group meetings to edit and formulate the bi-laws and at our next meeting these bi-laws were voted on along with the constitution of the organization. It was at this meeting too when the officers of the organization were nominated and voted on. It was my pleasure to serve as the first president of the Campus Police Investigators Association (CPIA). During the first year the CPIA grew in membership and included schools in Virginia and in Maryland. The following year I was reelected president and we sponsored several symposiums and still we grew in membership. Upon my retirement from Georgetown University the membership consisted of fourteen different universities and colleges. The Campus Law Enforcement Journal even did a story in one its issues about the CPIA.

I mentioned this about the CPIA because it has been a very valuable instrument in the closing of numerous cases involving more than one institution. One such case involved an individual, Gene Allison, who had somehow managed to get permission to set up a storage program for students belongings during the summer vacation. As it turned out this guy had entered into contracts with students from five of the different schools in the consortium (Georgetown, George Washington, Howard, American, and University of Maryland). The problem was, when the students came back to school and wanted to retrieve their belongings the nightmare began. Mr. Allison failed to maintain any decent records as to where an individuals belonging were stored and what type of belongings they were. He used four different storage facilities in Maryland and Virginia and was in arrears on the storage fees at three of the storage sites. This whole thing started when the students returned to school and wanted their belongings returned. It wasn't long after their return that we all started getting complaints about Mr. Allison's operation. An emergency meeting of the CPIA was called in order to discuss and come up with some sort of solution to this problem. All of the members got involved, even the ones whose students were affected by this shoddy operation. Granted, Mr. Allison had good intentions of storing the student's belongings at a very low rate, but, his plan backfired on him apparently from a lack of planning and poor record keeping on his part. It was decided to contact each of the storage facilities and explain to them what our situation was and after hearing our plight they were very cooperative. We then made arrangements with U-Haul for a cut rate on the rental of a couple of moving vans and we all went to the various storage sites and retrieved what belongings we could and took them to the students school. This was a time consuming operation and rather expensive, but, we were able to get almost all the belongings back to the students. Some were missing certain items like alarm clocks, radios, cassette players, etc., but, the contract they entered into with Mr. Allison did not provide any coverage for lost or missing items, so, they just had to take the loss and bite the bullet. We then arranged a meeting with one of the Assistant U. S. Attorneys in Superior Court and explained the whole thing to him and requested his advice in settling this matter. Consequently, each one of us who had students involved with this storage mess obtained warrants for Mr. Allison for various charges that included operating a business without a license, fraud, violating a minor's rights (none of the students were of legal age to enter into any contracts) and unlawful entry. The expenses for the truck rentals came out of the treasury of the CPIA and we were also suing Mr. Allison for those expenses. Mr. Allison was somewhat cooperative and had to take out a large loan to cover all these losses in order to keep from to jail. As it turned out the CPIA got its money back, the students were reimbursed for their lost and missing property and everybody was satisfied with the final outcome. Needless to say the students learned a very valuable lesson that wasn't taught in the classroom...before getting involved with a "save a buck" scheme they should first check with their campus police to insure they aren't getting taken for a ride.

Another interesting case involved the magazine salesperson coming on campus and getting the students to take out subscriptions for magazines. In one month our officers apprehended about twenty young people on the campus trying to sell these subscriptions and a lot of them were quite successful. These solicitors were warned of the Unlawful Entry statute, and were escorted off campus after taking their picture and preparing a field contact card on them and putting it on file. I contacted the other members of CPIA and they advised that they too were having a problem with magazine solicitors. While interrogating one of the solicitors I learned who their boss was, a Francois Versace, and I also found out where they were all staying. Their pitch to sell the subscriptions was that if an individual sold a certain amount of subscriptions they would receive specific prizes like a trip to Paris, or a computer, or a new car. Once I had gotten a complaint about them I initiated my investigation which lasted about three weeks. All these salespersons were staying at a motel in Falls Church, Virginia, so, I contacted the Falls Church Police Department and discussed my concern with one of the detectives of the Check and Fraud unit. He invited me to his office where he told me his department would cooperate in any way they could. I outlined to him my plan of action and he made the rest of the department aware of my presence and what was happening. I and another detective from the Falls Church Police went to the motel where Mr. Versace was staying and made contact with him. In no uncertain terms I explained to him the trouble he was in with his illegal selling techniques and the fact that he is subjecting his salespersons to arrest for trespassing and/or unlawful entry charges and soliciting without a license. I had his attention and told him that he had to come to my office with enough cash to buy back the subscriptions that had been sold at Georgetown University. When he asked why? I told him it was either that or I would get an arrest warrant for him. I had enough evidence against him to put him in jail for at least seven years. He informed me that it would take a couple of days to get that much money together and I informed him that it had to be tomorrow or the deal is off. I gave him my card and directions to my office and told him that I would be expecting him to be there before noon. With that, we left the room and as we were getting into the detectives car he told me "man, you are one tough dude! You didn't cut him any slack at all". I told him I didn't have that luxury when there is so much money involved and a reputation to protect. At about 10:45 the next day I got a call from the front desk that I had a visitor…it was Mr. Versace. I escorted him to my office where I produced all the subscriptions I had gotten from the students and we proceeded to get down to business. By the end of the day I had almost $3,000 in my desk earmarked for the various students whose subscriptions I had sold back to Mr. Versace. By 10:30pm that night the last student left my office with her money and a smile on her face. The following morning I contacted the other CPIA members and told them how I handled the situation and they couldn't believe that I got all that money back so fast. I also contacted the Falls Church Police and thanked the detectives who assisted me and told them what the outcome was. They in turn told me that they told Mr. Versace that he couldn't operate his business out of their town anymore and that he would have to move on and suggested that he might not want to come back to Falls Church, Virginia. I guess sometimes you have to really play hardball in dealing with some of the situations you come across. Other than our students being taken in on this type of operation it really galls me that someone like Versace will take these young kids, his sales persons, and fill their heads with ideas of getting some valuable prizes, but, neglecting to tell them about the legal aspects and ramifications of soliciting without a license. They are the ones who end up getting in a jam with the law, not Mr. Versace. There are many jurisdictions that take that quite seriously and will not hesitate a minute to impose a heavy fine on someone convicted of soliciting without a license. Fortunately, during my tenure that was the only case we had of that nature.

Occasionally rock concerts would be held at the McDonough Gymnasium and naturally that draws all the "goofies" in the area. Sometimes you can't believe your eyes when you see how these kids are dressed and their hair styles…purple hair, green hair, spiked hair, hair down to their knees, you name it and it appears at these concerts. Their actions almost make you laugh what with their slamming into each other and their gyrations. I often wonder what kind of parents these kids have. I have two boys and if either one of them started to leave our house dressed the way these kids were dressed, I'd tell them to keep on walking. Physical appearance to me is a very important thing and looking like you just got out of a paint barrel is not my idea of a mentally stable person regardless of their age. Maybe I'm just old fashioned, but, purple hair? Give me a break! There was a Patty Smith concert at the gym one time and during these concerts the ladies room always gets overworked...too many females and not enough stalls. At this particular concert two of the young females got into some sort of scuffle and I was the one who had to break it up. Believe me, I'd rather go into a den of lions rather than try to break up a fight between two women...if it's two guy involved you can punch them out, but with the female species it's a whole different ball game. At any rate I was somewhat successful in my effort and finally got them separated with only receiving a few scratches and a couple of minor slaps. When I found out what they were fighting about I felt like knocking them both out. It all started when they were both looking into the mirror in the ladies room and one of them made the comment "I look just Patty Smith" to which the other girl replied "like hell you do". That was it! To be perfectly honest with you I think Patty Smith had about as much sex appeal as a left over lima bean, then again that's just my opinion. While the two combatants were cooling down I made contact with one of the concert security guys and had him meet with me. I told him about this incident and turned the two girls over to him. He escorted them to the door and made them leave the concert. As I was tied up with this situation, Jeff Horton, my partner, was involved with a few drunk (or high) kids. I responded to his location to assist and upon my arrival one of the individuals started running his mouth and was swearing up a blue streak. I told him to watch his language and cool down, but he replied with more profanity and a reference to my maternal ancestry. At this point I'd had enough of these young jerks that didn't know how to act in a public place, so, I grabbed this guy by his shirt front and slammed him against the wall and told him if he opened his mouth one more time I'd rip his face off and spit down his throat. That got his attention along with the other guys that were involved. Jeff told them how lucky that young man was because the last time someone got me mad he ended up in traction for five weeks. All of a sudden things quieted down and we led all of them out the door and had them escorted off campus by a couple of uniformed officers.

Needless to say, I was never too thrilled about having to work the various concerts...especially the rock groups. There was always some sort of trouble involved with them. Once there was an outdoor concert and we kept getting flooded with phone calls complaining about the volume of the music (I use the term music for want of a better word) and no matter how many times we told the band to turn down their amplifiers and woofers and what all, but, the complaints just kept on rolling in. I even told the band leader that if he didn't comply and keep the noise down I would shut off the power and cancel the concert. I can't recall how many times I had prayed for rain that night. It even got to the point where the Metropolitan Police responded to the complaints. The MPD officers could see that we were making every effort to control the volume, but, it was an exercise in futility. One of the MPD Sergeants got the band leader and told him if the volume got above the legal level of their noise monitor they would shut down the concert. We all hung around for about fifteen minutes and the next thing you know the band is playing so loud I thought the needle on the monitor was going to snap off. The MPD Sergeant found the power source and started pulling plugs and in a New York minute there was total silence. Then the audience started yelling and carrying on and additional

MPD units had to be called for crowd control. It took us almost two hours and a few skirmishes with some of the attendees before we could get everyone out of the area and off the campus. It goes without saying that the concert security guys were about as helpful as two dead flies. They did almost nothing to assist with the crowd control and monitoring the audience.

One winter we had another concert in the gym and as usual all the freaks showed up dressed in their nutty clothes with their weird hair styles and their faces all made up. Believe me, it was really a sight to see. It was during this concert that we made a couple of good drug busts. I was dressed in casual clothes and as we were circulating through the crowd one guy asked me "hey man, want some good stuff"? I told him yes and we got out of the crowd. I was able to give Jeff the high sign and he followed us outside to make the deal. The dealer took me to his car in the parking lot and asked me how much did I want? I told him as much as he had and he handed me three baggies of marijuana and as I acted as though I was reaching for my wallet I pulled out my badge case, identified myself and placed him under arrest. Jeff was right there and helped me place him in handcuffs because he was not at all happy about the turn of events. MPD was called for a transport and they also confiscated the dealer's car as contraband.

That was the first arrest that night and went as smooth as silk…not all of them are that easy. The next one was little harder and Jeff was the buyer this time. It was about an hour later when Jeff was approached. Jeff and the dealer went to the men's room briefly and then proceeded to the parking lot. I followed closely behind and acted as though I'd had too much to drink and couldn't find my car. Just as the deal took place and Jeff was making the arrest, the suspect bolted and started to run, but, he came running in my direction, so, I took out my badge and held it up for the suspect to see and told him to freeze or I'd blow him away as I reached for my handcuffs. He thought I was reaching for a gun and stopped dead in his tracks. You should have seen the look on his face when he found out later that I wasn't armed. To add to his woes that night when we searched him for weapons pursuant to the arrest I noticed that he was wearing motorcycle boots, so, just to be on the safe side we had him take off his boots. We were standing in about two inches of snow and naturally he protested, but, an Arlington County police officer was shot and killed by someone who had hidden a gun inside his boot. We told him that if he didn't comply we would remove them ourselves and only God knows what condition they would be in after we got them off. He took them off and it took us at least fifteen minutes to inspect them for any other contraband or possible weapons. All this time the suspect was standing in the snow and then we placed him in our cruiser and took him to the O'Gara Building and called MPD again for another transport and vehicle confiscation. When MPD did an inventory of the suspects vehicle after it was impounded they found all kinds of drugs; cocaine, marijuana, some LSD, and a lot of paraphernalia, which the possession of, is a violation in the District of Columbia. The next day Mr. Lamb called me and Jeff into his office and told us that Lieutenant Sarnie of the Second District had called him and told him what a good Jeff and I had done and he added his gratitude also. In all honesty it was a good night, but, a real long one too as I didn't get home that night until about 2:30am…but, it was worth it.

While we are on the subject of illegal drugs we had a situation that blew a lot of peoples minds. As I had mentioned earlier my office had the responsibility of all lost and found items. As the school year was drawing to a close I had one of my investigators, Dee Faulkner, sort through the items we had and make the necessary preparations for the disposal of the unclaimed and unidentifiable property. In the interest of saving time on Friday afternoon as he was leaving work Dee took it upon himself to take the unclaimed book bags home with him in an attempt to identify the owners if possible.

On Saturday afternoon I got a call from Dee advising me that after going through several book bags he came upon one book bag that had a rotten banana, two moldy sandwiches and some clear plastic baggies with some unknown substances in them. He also informed me that there were numerous other suspicious items in the bag. I told him to secure the bag and bring it into the office on Monday morning. On Monday I opened the bag to see what type of items were in there and when I did I suggested to Mr. Lamb that we open the bag in his office with the door closed and locked. When we emptied out the book bag we discovered there were enough illegal drugs to place the entire D.C. population on a high. We immediately contacted MPD and two detectives from the Narcotics Unit responded along with their various field test kits. In one bag there was about a pound of heroin which the detectives said was 90% pure. Another bag held a pound of cocaine which was 85% pure. There were fifty strips of paper that was two feet long and two inches wide that contained loads of LSD dots. There were three baggies of marijuana and several medicine bottles that contained various types of "uppers", "downers", and other barbiturates. Neither the detectives nor we could imagine how someone could be as careless and lose a bag like this. There was no way of identifying the owner of the book bag nor was there any way to determine if it belonged to a student or an outsider who may have been visiting the campus. It appears that the book bag was lost by someone who was to deliver it to some other person or persons. At any rate, I would have hated to have been in the delivery person's shoes when the recipient found out that the book bag had been lost. There's no telling where he or she might have ended up…maybe where the Potomac River empties out. The total worth of the contents of that bag was estimated to be between $700,000 and $800,000. All the drugs were boxed up and turned over to the MPD detectives after they signed a receipt for the property.

Check and fraud cases were my favorite cases to work. With these sorts of cases you have some physical evidence to work with. One such case involved the parent of one of our students. One day I received a phone call from the Dean of Admissions wanting me to come to his office to discuss a rather sensitive matter. Upon my arrival I was informed that several checks that had been written to the school by Mr. Thomas Herndon had been returned for non sufficient funds. These checks were for pretty high amounts of money and the dean didn't wanted to know the best way to approach this situation without causing any undue embarrassment to either the parent or the student. I advised him that I would handle the matter as tactfully as possible and would keep him abreast of the progress. I contacted Mr. Herndon by telephone as he lived in Philadelphia and suggested that we meet in person to discuss these returned checks. Mr. Herndon stated that wouldn't be necessary as he was going to check with his bank to determine why these checks were returned and also he was going to send us a cashier check to cover the returned checks. One week went by and no cashier check had yet been received, so, I made contact with Mr. Herndon again and he advised me that his business schedule had kept him from getting to the bank and taking care of this matter. At this point I reminded Mr. Herndon the gravity of the situation and suggested that he take the necessary action to resolve this problem as soon as possible. He agreed and stated that he would take care of things that same day. Another week went by and still no check, but, he did appear at the Admissions Office to speak with the dean. The dean called me and asked me to sit in on their meeting to which I agreed. At this meeting Mr. Herndon stated that he had been to his bank and he explained that this whole mess was caused by some book keeping error on the part of the bank and that the bank was supposed to send us a letter of explanation. The story he told was rather unbelievable, but, as a parent myself I gave him the benefit of the doubt. Mr. Herndon further requested that he be given a little additional time to get things straightened out with his bank in Philadelphia. The dean was gracious enough to give Mr. Herndon a thirty day extension with the provision that if this matter wasn't resolved to the satisfaction of the University legal action would have to be taken. After the thirty day period expired we were still at square one with no corrective action taken whatsoever on Mr. Herndon's part. Consequently, it became necessary to contact the student, Julia Herndon, and inform her that she would have to withdraw from school as her tuition and board plan had not been paid. Ms. Herndon was shocked and totally confused about the situation and it became necessary to explain to her the reason for this action. Needless to say Mr. Herndon was extremely upset over this action and I told him that he left us no alternative and that we had been more than generous with him with time to set matters straight. Mr. Herndon ranted and raved for about ten minutes on the phone at which point I just hung up, waited fifteen minutes and called him back and asked him if he was in a calmer state of mind to which he answered yes. I then told him he had one last opportunity to make things right or I would have to obtain a warrant for his arrest for uttering a worthless check. He told me to do whatever I had to do, so, that afternoon I went to the Judge in Chambers office with my prepared affidavit and swore to its contents, had it signed and then proceeded to the warrant office where I had the arrest warrant issued. Inasmuch as the amount of money involved was in excess of $20,000 a felony warrant was issued. A copy of the warrant was sent to the Philadelphia Police Department and the U. S. Marshal's Office in Philadelphia.

About two weeks later I received a call from the Assistant U.S. Attorney's office in Philadelphia stating that I was needed in Philadelphia that afternoon for an extradition hearing for Mr. Thomas Herndon. I advised the caller that this was very short notice and that I wasn't even aware that Mr. Herndon had been arrested. I told Mr. Lamb about the call and he had the Watch Commander drive me to the Metro Station where I was fortunate enough to be able catch a train to Philadelphia. Upon arriving in Philadelphia I caught a cab to the courthouse and made it to the respective courtroom just in time. The attorney for Mr. Herndon requested a postponement for another date and I almost hit the ceiling. The Assistant U. S. Attorney argued against this request and it was denied to my relief. That was one hell of a hassle to get there on time and I wasn't about to have to make that trip again. The hearing went as scheduled and Mr. Herndon was extradited back to the District of Columbia for trial. The reason why the

U. S. Attorney's office was involved was because the crimes took place in the District of Columbia making it a federal case. This case finally went to trial and Mr. Herndon was found guilty of five counts of fraud and one count of theft of services. The University wasn't out for blood and settled for half of what Mr. Herndon owed and was awarded $10,000. The only person that got hurt out of this ordeal was Julia Herndon…having to withdraw from school and be embarrassed by her father's actions.

Sean Edwards was some sort of character that could almost charm a bird out of a tree. And he was always ready with an answer for everything. My first contact with him was over some books from Lauinger Library that were way overdue with fines totaling sixty five dollars. Sean was not a student of Georgetown University, but, he did have a borrower's card for Lauinger Library. He had an address listed in Arlington, Virginia but that turned out to be a vacant lot, so, the only way to contact him was to wait until he returned to the campus. With his red hair and physical description he was not hard to spot if he appeared and all of our officers were made aware of my wanting to talk with him. About a week later Sean appeared at, of all places, Lauinger Library. I got a radio call from our officer on that beat and I immediately responded to the library where I saw Sean. Sean was a pretty good size man and not knowing anything about him, other than being a deadbeat, I radioed for some backup just in case. After the backup arrived I had them stand by and I approached Sean, showed him my badge, identified myself, and asked him to accompany me to my office. He agreed and didn't provide any resistance.

Once in my office and with a witness present I read Sean the Miranda warning and had him sign and initial it. I told Sean we wanted the money for the overdue books and we wanted the books returned. Sean said he was out of a job at that time, but, he would bring the books back the next day. I told Sean that wasn't good enough and that I would drive him to his residence and get the books now. Sean said that he didn't have the books at his residence and that it would take a few days to get them all together. We're talking about fifteen books on as many subjects. Further questioning resulted in the books being sold to a few local old book stores. The more I talked to Sean the more I got to dislike him and the shorter my temper got. After almost two hours with Sean I was ready to rip his face off, but, I maintained my composure and made him tell me where he was living which happened to be a dingy room in Arlington. I advised Sean that I wanted to see his room to see if he had any other Georgetown property there. Sean signed

Consent to Search form and we proceeded to his room in Arlington. There wasn't much to the room, a bed, a chair, and a small table. He didn't have much of a wardrobe either, but, he did have a suit. I did find three books that belonged to the university and I confiscated them. I made Sean give me the names of the book stores that bought the library books and we visited all of them. I identified myself to the owners and showed them my credentials and they were most cooperative by removing the respective books from their shelves and placing them in a separate location where they could be safeguarded from sale. The amount of cash involved to buy these books back totaled $400.00 which Sean did not have. I told Sean he had one week to come up with the money or I was going to get a warrant for him for theft of library property which in the District is considered a felony. As the end of the week drew nigh, Sean appeared at my office wearing a tuxedo and all shaved and as clean as the board of the health. He advised me that he couldn't raise the money owed this week because of not having a job, so I asked him how he could afford a tuxedo and his answer was that it had been provided him by his new employer and he was on his way to work at that time. Sean said that he wanted to assure me that as soon as he got his first paycheck he would come to my office with the money he owed and never return to the Georgetown University campus again. Being the gentleman that I am I gave Sean a two week extension with the strong warning that was the end of it. No more stalling. At the end of those two weeks I never saw hide or hair of Sean so I proceeded with obtaining a warrant for his arrest. With that warrant in hand I and Detective Rose from Second District went to Sean's place of employment and very ceremoniously placed him under arrest, put him in handcuffs and escorted him out of the restaurant where he had been working. Sean's face was just as red as a tomato as he was led away. Sean was patted down pursuant to the arrest, but, no weapons were found on him and he was then transported to the Second District for processing to the Central Cell Block. Two months after Sean was taken into custody he appeared before Judge Nick Nunzio (a terrific judge...a cop's judge) and received a sentence of three years confinement plus a $1,000 fine. After that trial I never saw or heard of Sean Edwards again, which I might add, was a blessed relief.

When making an arrest in the District of Columbia there is a lot of paper work involved and a lot of time is wasted at the U.S. Attorney's Office in the Superior Court. There is a process to be followed in order to take the perpetrator to trial and this is called "papering a case" or just plain "papering". This is a rather complex procedure too and you have to make sure all your "i's" are dotted and all your "t"s" are crossed. When you arrive with your copies of the Arrest Report and the signed and initialed PD Forms 47, Miranda Warnings there are several other forms to be filled out and after that is completed you sit and wait to review the case with an Assistant U. S. Attorney (AUSA) who will determine if the case has merit to go to trial. In the event your case doesn't meet their criteria to be heard in court it is called a "no paper" meaning that the AUSA reviewing the case won't go forward with it. His decision is not etched in stone and can be protested with the Chief AUSA. Such was the situation that happened with me a couple of times when I had some slam dunk cases. John Finnegan was the Chief AUSA at that time and after reviewing one of my cases he told me it was damn good case and for me to take it back to the reviewing AUSA that decided to no paper it and tell him to "paper the damn thing!" Situations like this can create some resentment between you and the AUSA as they hate to have their feathers ruffled. Not all AUSA's are like that. As a matter of fact I had established a pretty good rapport with a couple of them and they knew that I didn't come all the way down there to paper a bad case. They knew I had all my ducks in a row when I showed up at their office to paper a case. One time as I was papering a case I noticed this particular ring that the AUSA was wearing and I mentioned how much it looked like a Super Bowl ring. The AUSA, Mike Hull, said that's what it was and handed it to me to look at. Mike had been Number 66 with the Washington Redskins when they won the Super Bowl. A football injury ended his career and he went to law school, got his degree, and became an AUSA. Ever since that first meeting Mike and I became pretty friendly and whenever I had a case to paper and Mike saw me he would slip me in ahead of a lot of other guy's. There is so much milling around in that area no one even noticed it. At any rate, what with all this paper work involved with an arrest some officers would skate around making a collar (arrest). Of course those officers didn't see many promotions or pay raises either and were sort of looked down on by the other cops.

The consortium of the universities in the D.C. area developed their own academy for the training of campus police officers. Due to my expertise of papering cases I was designated to instruct classes on this subject in addition to proper arrest procedures and procedures for obtaining search warrants and arrest warrants. In the course of making my lesson plans I thought it would be a good idea for the academy students to be very familiar with the various criminal laws of the District of Columbia. I screened my copy of the D. C. Criminal Code and culled out those particular violations that would be pertinent to campus police officers and typed a list of these violations along with their code numbers and descriptions of the violations and the maximum possible sentence for each violation. This information was a handy tool to have available because some MPD officers considered the campus police officer's as a little inferior to them in experience and knowledge of the law and some of them would argue against making a transport to their particular district headquarters. With this violation information in hand the MPD officer can be shown where all the elements of the arrest are present and he has no grounds for argument. I've been there and had to convince the transporting MPD officer that it was a good arrest and a case for prosecution. After a couple of go arounds with a few of the MPD officer's concerning transporting a prisoner the word got around and they finally realized that "Hey, Sergeant Christian knows what the hell he's talking about!"

These courses that I taught only consumed one or two days a month so as not to interfere with my primary function of investigating crimes.

Two of the most dreaded crimes that could occur on any campus are murder and sex offenses. Fortunately we never experienced a homicide on campus, but, it was a sad, sad day when we did have a female sophomore student murdered off campus while working in a jewelry store on Wisconsin Avenue in the District. The student had only been working at the store for about three months when this perpetrator attempted to rob the place and for no apparent reason shot and killed the female student. The suspect was apprehended, tried, convicted, and sentenced to thirty years in prison, but, with the parole system as it is in the District of Columbia I would venture that this gutless, worthless piece of trash is out now walking the streets and committing more robberies and murders. I wish I could say that we didn't have any sex offenses on campus too, but, that would stretching the truth. In this regard though, for as big as the campus is and considering the population of the campus there really were only a couple of cases that come to mind. One such case a female student called our department at about 8:00pm one night from an on campus emergency phone and stated that she had been sexually assaulted behind the Animal Vivarium in the medical center complex. I was working late catching up on some paper work and filing cases when the call came in so I and a female officer responded to where the victim was to interview her and get what information we could as far as a description of the suspect for an

APB (all points bulletin). Upon our arrival the victim did not seem the least bit distraught or virtually shaken up. We went to the exact location that this attack took place and as soon as we got there I felt a strange feeling growing inside me. This was in the fall of the year and the victim was wearing one of those sweater type jackets yet there were no leaves on her apparel. There were a few other things that didn't appear to fit such as her hair not being messed up and no smearing of her make up. I questioned her for quite some length as to how she managed to be in this particular area inasmuch as it is pretty well isolated from the rest of the campus. The victim stated that she had been jogging and was taking a short cut back to the main campus when her attacker jumped out from behind some bushes and grabbed her and threw her down on the ground and raped her. When I told her we would have to go to the hospital for the medical people to gather evidence she declined to go stating she was afraid of hospitals. All of a sudden lights started to flash inside my head telling me this alleged victim was lying through her teeth. At this point I called the dispatcher to have a sex crime unit of MPD respond to our location and when the student heard this call she began to panic and fall apart and grabbed my arm and said she didn't want any other police involved. After about another half hour of questioning her she finally admitted that she had not been attacked. When asked why she made up this story she said she just wanted some attention. I cancelled the APB and the request for a sex crime unit and we took the student to my office where she was given her Miranda rights with the female officer present. I explained to the student the penalties for filing a false police report and I also explained to her the options open for her...being arrested and taken downtown or facing the Student Adjudication Board. She opted for the adjudication and prior to leaving my office I gave her a severe lecture for her actions and what sort of consequences could have come form them. Needless to say she was very much in tears when she went back to her residence hall room.

About three weeks after "move in day" when the upper class students all returned and the freshmen students got settled into their new living quarters a female student who was living in the New South residence hall which was just across the street from our offices came rushing in and reported that someone had entered her room while she was taking a nap and was feeling all over. She woke up and the intruder fled her room before she had a chance to get a good description of him. She was able to tell us that he was rather stout or chubby and was wearing some dark green pants. This happened at about 2:00pm in the afternoon of a school day, so, I immediately responded to New South and met with Jack DeGioia, the Resident Director (who now is the President of Georgetown University) and advised him about this incident. I questioned about thirty students to see if I could obtain some information that could be of use, but came up empty handed. The next morning after the shift changed I went back to New South to snoop around and when I looked inside a trash container on the third floor I found a pair of dark green pants that someone had apparently thrown away. I took these pants down to my office and labeled them as possible evidence then I returned to New South and started questioning the residents of the third floor to see if anyone happened to see who might have discarded those pants. I got the name of a possible suspect and went to his room, knocked on the door and identified myself. The student, Jeff Markley, opened the door and I could see that he was rather portly and could lose some weight. I showed him my badge, asked if I could enter his room, and told him I wanted to have a chat with him. As soon as he saw my badge he started to get jittery and nervous. I asked him what size pants did he wear and when he told me it was the same size pants that I had found in the trash container. I asked him if he had thrown away any pants and he said that he had because he no longer liked them. At this point I summoned another investigator, Jim McNally, to meet me in this room and when he arrived I advised the student of his Miranda rights and told him that he was a suspect in a case of Burglary I and Simple Assault. Upon hearing this Jeff broke down in tears and admitted to being in the complainant's room and touching her. He said that he couldn't help himself, that he was compelled to do what he did. With this information we escorted Jeff to my office and contacted Jack Degoia and advised him of our actions. Jack came to my office and offered whatever assistance he could provide and we both discussed the case with Mr. Lamb in his office so he could make the determination as how to proceed with the case. It was pretty evident that Jeff needed some psychiatric help, so, we left it up to the Dean of Student Affairs to make the final decision as to the disposition of the case. Jeff was suspended from school and his parents were advised as to what had happened. They came to the university and Jeff was released into their custody with the written stipulation that he gets medical help or an arrest warrant for Jeff would be obtained. They were also advised that this matter would be closely monitored for compliance and any violation of the stipulations would render the custody agreement null and void. The victim and her parents were contacted by the Dean and advised of the action taken and they were quite satisfied with what had been done. About a week later I received a package in the mail containing a beautiful pen and pencil set. The parents of the victim enclosed a short note thanking me for my efforts. I told Mr. Lamb about the gift and asked him what I should do with it as I am not supposed to accept gifts or gratuities for doing my job and he told me to "…keep it, you deserve it for a job well done."

After the Spring break in 1987 one of the female students that I knew from past encounters, Rose Wilson, called the department and asked to speak with me. When I answered the phone she told me that she was calling from her room and that she had just been raped. I and a female officer immediately responded to her room to take the necessary information and take her to the emergency room of the hospital for them to collect the necessary evidence to substantiate a charge of rape. Rose was a very helpful victim and even provided the name of the perpetrator who happened to be the boyfriend of her roommate. There was a bit of a problem though, Larry Lang, the suspect, was a member of the basketball team. As a matter of fact, he was the top scorer of the team. Needless to say I knew I was in for a rough ride in order to do anything to a basketball player, but, what's right is right and the chips just had to lie where they fell. I obtained a written statement from Rose and then returned to the hospital and got the needed medical report and the evidence of her examination to support her charges. According to Rose, she had returned a day early from Spring break and as she was unpacking her suitcases and settling back into her room Larry came by looking for her roommate. They engaged in a short conversation about their Spring break activities and then Larry began to make sexual advances on Rose who rejected them and asked him to leave the room. Larry refused to leave and forced Rose down on her bed against her will and protests. He managed to do what he wanted and then told Rose not to tell anyone about what happened. I then proceeded to the Athletic Coordinators Office in an attempt to have them contact Larry Lang so I could get a statement from him and question him about this matter. As expected, I got the verbal run around and was told that they would call me as soon they were able to contact him. At that point I advised them of the seriousness of the matter and wouldn't tolerate any stalling. I also informed them that I had sufficient evidence to obtain an arrest warrant if that occurred. As soon as I left that office everyone must have gotten on their phones and made all sorts of calls because about ten minutes later I was summoned to Mr. Lamb's office where I was told that he was directed by higher authority to take control of this investigation. I handed all my reports and evidence over to Mr. Lamb along with my badge and ID card. Mr. Lamb refused to accept my badge and ID card and explained to me that being that this was a very sensitive case the administration felt that he should conduct the investigation to avoid any adverse publicity for the basketball team and the university. I expressed my feelings about their decision and suggested a few itineraries for them and left his office with my badge and ID card still on Mr. Lamb's desk. I think that the basketball team got more protection than the President of the United States. The next day when I returned to clean out my desk I found my badge and ID card lying on my desk with a note for me to see Mr. Lamb. I knocked on his door and as we met over coffee he urged me to reconsider and stay with the department. I gave it some serious thought and decided that I had too many years invested on this job not to stick it out, so, I agreed and went on about my business. As it turned out with Rose's case it never went to trial. As a matter of fact there was never an arrest made and Rose is practicing medicine now somewhere thanks to her free education and graduating from the Georgetown University Medical School. It's amazing the lengths that some of these schools will go to just to protect their prized athletes.

While on the subject of sex offenses, every campus police department harbors the fear that a rape might happen on their campus. Our department also had that fear, so, I developed a rape prevention program, and I presented this program at least two times every semester. I made it a point to have interesting guest speakers from the Rape Crisis Center, MPD Sex Offense Branch, and various other agencies that dealt with these matters. There would always be refreshments and plenty of publicity well in advance about the programs. We had two campus newspapers on campus; The Hoya and The Georgetown Voice and they willingly ran notices about the presentations of the program and the campus radio station, WGTB also made public announcements about the presentations. Everyone on campus knew about the programs and their availability. BUT, out of a female student population of approximately 2,500 only about ten or fifteen would attend any of these programs. Believe me, it got to be quite discouraging, and after a couple of years I suggested to Mr. Lamb that we just discontinue with the programs due to a lack of interest on the part of the students. Mr. Lamb decided against it and said that as long as we present the programs we couldn't justifiably be criticized if one of our female students did end up being raped. I agreed and continued with my efforts in futility.

In the course of my duties I had attended a rape prevention seminar in Newark, Delaware where Jessica Savitch, a Philadelphia TV news personality, was the guest speaker and had done a series about street crime and rape. At the conclusion of the seminar I spoke with Ms. Savitch and asked her about the possibility of borrowing some of her material for a new rape prevention program that I was planning. She agreed and we set up a time and date for me to come to Philadelphia to pick up the material at the TV station. In the interim there was a very severe oil refinery fire in Philadelphia that claimed the lives of several Philadelphia fire fighters and, as luck would have it, the day I was to go to pick up the material from Ms. Savitch was the same day that they were having about seven or eight funerals for the deceased fire fighters and numerous streets were blocked off and there were detours all over town. I managed to get the rape prevention material from Ms. Savitch and what with all the detours and me not being all familiar with Philadelphia I accidentally got turned around and found myself somewhere in South Philadelphia. It was summer time and having no air conditioning in my car I had the windows rolled all the way down for some fresh air. As I was stopped at a red traffic light waiting for it to change green, a car pulled up beside me carrying about five or six black males.

The one sitting in the passenger seat yelled over to me "Hey M….. F….., how would you like to have your car turned over"? I aimed my Rossi .38 caliber snub nose out the window at him and yelled back "How would you like to be the next dude to die in this town"? With that, they didn't even wait for the light to change green and they must have burnt rubber for three blocks just to get away from me. A couple of blocks later I saw a sign for Interstate 95 and a few minutes later I was out of that town and headed back to my office.

Every year there was a dedication ceremony in which the Robert Kennedy Humanitarian Award was presented to some earning individual. Senator Ted Kennedy presented this award and normally there was a lot of pomp and circumstance involved with this dedication ceremony. Needless to say security measures were strengthened and there was much coordination between my office and the Kennedy security detail of the Secret Service. This ceremony was always held in the auditorium of Copley Hall. At the main entrance of Copley Hall the first step that is about three inches high and could be a safety hazard if you weren't aware of its existence. At one particular ceremony I was detailed at these steps when the Kennedy party arrived in their limousine. Ted Kennedy got out first, went up about three steps, and started talking to some other person concerning the speech he was going to give at the presentation. Rose Kennedy was the next person to leave the limo and she started to ascend the stairs, but not knowing about that first step she tripped on it and started to fall toward the steps. I was able to grab her and keep her from kissing the steps when all of a sudden the Senator decided to give some attention to his mother and came to where we were and took his mother's arm and told me that he could take care of her and then they proceeded up the steps. At least Rose Kennedy did thank me for my efforts, but not one word of thanks from the Senator. Actually, knowing what I knew about Mr. Kennedy, I really wasn't expecting any sign of appreciation. During another one of these events I was assigned to the Copley Hall roadway to keep the vehicular traffic from jamming up while people were exiting their cars at the Copley steps. As one vehicle approached I signaled the driver to halt the vehicle but he kept coming, so, I signaled him again to stop and he still refused. I, being the idiot that I am, stepped out in front of the car and the driver finally stopped. Even though I was in plain clothes I had my badge very prominently displayed and I went to the driver side door and the driver rolled down his window and I asked him if he was a native born American and did he understand the word "stop". He answered yes to both questions and then asked me if I knew whom he was to which I replied "I don't know and I don't care if you are Saint Peter, when I tell you to stop you stop." That is when he very pompously told me that he was Sargent Shriver to which I replied "that's nice, but, when you're told to stop by an officer you stop or you'll get locked up." At that point Mr. Lamb arrived and asked if there was a problem and I told him not any more and Mr. Shriver drove off, red face and all and mad as hell. I guess no one else had ever spoken to him in that manner before and I was half expecting to be getting some form of letter of reprimand, but, none ever came to my office. Believe me, every year I dreaded those ceremonies as the least I had to do with the Kennedy's the better I liked it. Some of the ones that I had met weren't all that bad. Eunice and Ethel Kennedy were very personable and Marie Shriver was completely the opposite of her father.

Georgetown University has hosted its share of noted personalities and as such I had the opportunity to meet all of them. When the Jewish Student Alliance invited Abba Eban, Prime Minister of Israel, to speak at the university I and Jeff Horton were his body guards along with his own security. Mr. Eban was a very charming and appreciative person and thanked Jeff and me personally for our services.

Ted Turner was another real nice guy and with all of his millions of dollars he didn't talk down to you (like certain other people from New England I've had the displeasure of dealing with) and joked around. It baffles me how he ever got mixed up with the likes of Jane Fonda. Well as the saying goes "to each his own".

John Glenn, the former astronaut, visited Georgetown University when he was campaigning for the Vice President position and I had the opportunity to shake his hand and get his autograph (two, one for each of my sons). He too was a very pleasant person.

Margaret Thatcher, while the Prime Minister of England, was visiting the White House and came to the university for an informal discussion with the students and faculty of the School of Foreign Service. Inasmuch as I and Jeff Horton were assigned to her personal security we were in a position to talk with her. She was a very charming lady.

The Dalai Lama of Tibet also paid us a visit, however, he was only on the campus for about an hour, and even though there was somewhat of a language barrier I had the opportunity to speak with him briefly and shake his hand.

One year the Law School had its graduating ceremonies at the Daughters of the American Revolution (DAR) hall. The guest speaker was Elizabeth Dole who at that time was the Secretary of Transportation. Pete Pervi and I had the pleasure of providing security for her too and as such I had the chance to talk with her briefly and tell her how I admired her husband for his stand on the religious cults. Mrs. Dole was a very warm person and as congenial as could be. It was a real pleasure to be in her presence.

William Windom portrays a doctor in the TV series "Murder She Wrote" and had a daughter attending Georgetown University. One evening, due to the heavy traffic across Key Bridge, I decided to wait it out and went to the Center Pub for a little libation. As I was standing at the bar I noticed a gentleman at the end of the bar near the windows. I asked him if he was William Windom and he said he was and we got into a conversation that lasted almost an hour during which time we bought each other a drink. Mr. Windom was a real down to earth person and not the least bit phony or haughty and never gave the impression that he was better than you.

I came in contact with the Reverend Jesse Jackson during the problems we were having with apartheid demonstrations which will be addressed later.

Nelson Rockefeller was also another personable individual who, with all his millions of dollars and power, couldn't have been a nicer person to be around.

He too treated us with the same respect that we gave him and was very appreciative of our efforts to provide him with the best possible security coverage.

Former Secretary of State Jean Kirkpatrick was an adjunct professor in the School of Foreign Service and as such was on campus quite frequently. In view of her status we were detailed to provide her with security, however, she was of the opinion that it wasn't necessary as she really wasn't a controversial person. She got the security anyway unbeknownst to her and once during her tenure she approached me and said, "I know who you are"! I replied that I was glad she knew and whether she liked it or not we were there for her. She smiled and thanked me and that was the end of any debate about security for her. She just accepted the fact that we were concerned for her safety and security. Every once in a while she would throw us a wave and a smile.

Henry Kissinger was another adjunct professor for the School of Foreign Service and for some reason was a rather controversial figure as opposed to Jean Kirkpatrick. On one rare occasion he and one of the Secret Service Agents assigned to him drove to the campus in his personal car to deliver a lecture in the formal lounge of Copley Hall. At that time there was a lot of unrest with many of the students for one reason or another. Actually, students can find some of the dumbest things to get all worked up about and only God knows what their problem is. While Mr. Kissinger was giving his lecture I noticed a large group of students surrounding his car and shouting about all different things that was unintelligible. I advised Mr. Lamb of this and I suggested that rather than run a gauntlet (so to speak) with Mr. Kissinger I could get my car from the parking lot and enter through the Reservoir Road entrance and drive it to the fire exit door of the lounge in Copley Hall. That way we could take Mr. Kissinger out the fire escape and into my car and take him where he wanted to go without having to deal with a bunch of rowdy students. Mr. Lamb agreed that it was an excellent plan; so, I left Copley Hall, got my car, and ended up waiting for Mr. Kissinger to exit the building. After about fifteen minutes the fire exit door opened and out came Mr. Kissinger and his bodyguard. I had the rear door already opened and all they had to do was get in and we drove away. Once off campus Mr. Kissinger stated that he would like to be driven to his town house in the Georgetown area so that is where I took them. Upon leaving the car Mr. Kissinger expressed his deep gratitude and must have thanked me a dozen times. Ever since that time whenever Mr. Kissinger would see me on campus he would make it a point to say hello and ask about my family.

I have no clue as to who made the decision to have the noted atheist Madelyn Murray O'Hare visit the university, but there she was in the Hall of Nations with her mouth like a sewer. Despite her reputation her appearance on the campus did draw a certain amount of attendance. I think most people attended her presentation out of curiosity…I think they wanted to see the woman with the "foulest mouth in the world" or to see of she really had two heads. I was assigned to provide her with security so I had to cover her presentation where she vehemently put down organized religion, faith in God, prayer and in general just ridiculed everyone who believed in a superior being. Personally, I couldn't wait for her to shut her mouth and get the hell off campus and I dreaded the idea that I had to provide her with much needed protection until she was gone. She had everyone really fired up and ready to tear her to shreds and a lot of those in attendance got up and left the room. I will give credit to a lot of the students who, during her presentation, stood up and turned their backs to her for about five minutes before leaving the room. By the time she had finished saying what she wanted to say there were about ten people left in the room. And to put the icing on the cake it didn't phase her one bit. When we departed the Hall of Nations in the Walsh Building there was a crowd of students, faculty, and staff waiting outside that booed and jeered her as I escorted her to her waiting car. Once I saw her car turn the corner of 36th Street and Prospect Avenue I drew a breath of relief and said a short prayer for the Lord giving me the patience and restraint from choking her to death. Oh well, I guess it takes all kinds of people to make a world, but, we could well do without her kind. Meeting people like her makes me love my dogs all the more.

Gerald Ford has been known for not being the most graceful person on earth and after his term as President of the United States when he visited Georgetown University it became a proven fact. There was some type of a big function on campus involving Mr. Ford which was followed by a formal dinner in the Faculty Lounge of Copley Hall. There were eight large round tables set up with seating for eight people per table. Those tables really looked nice with beautiful center pieces on the lace table cloths, real fancy china and stemmed glass ware with some filled with water. There was also a portable bar set up and everyone was sipping some type of liquid refreshment. Gerald Ford was mingling with the guests for about twenty minutes or more and as he approached my position he decided to place his drink on one of the tables to adjust his necktie. I was only about ten feet away from him and he smiled at me and we both nodded to each other. After adjusting his tie he reached for his drink on the table and just as he touched the glass the table collapsed on one side and everything went to the floor, not to mention that it made one hell of a racket. Naturally everybody looked in that direction and there stood Mr. Ford, all by himself looking as sheepish as possible. I felt very sorry for that man as it really wasn't his fault, but, with his reputation for being klutzy I knew what everybody was thinking. The caterers got the mess cleaned up in record time and the table all set up again. As it turned out it happened to be the fault of the caterers because whoever put the tables up didn't secure the sliding locking mechanism and it was just a matter of time before it gave way. Until I die I'll never forget the look on Mr. Ford's face as though to say "Oh God, not again". For some unknown reason Mr. Ford came over to me and shook my hand and said "…at least no one was sitting at the table to have their salad in their lap." We both laughed and he walked away. After that incident the rest of the evening went smoothly with no more mishaps.

Georgetown University has a terrific School of Foreign Service and as such foreign heads of state very often visits the university. One such visit was that of the Shah of Iran when he was in Washington with meetings at the White House. The word of his impending visit to the campus brought out thousands of Iranian protestors who picketed the campus for three days prior to his arrival. These protests required extra security to insure none of the protestors penetrated the campus grounds, consequently, all days off were cancelled and all shifts were placed on twelve-hour status. These protestors filled the streets and sidewalks with their signs, chanting and jeering. Additional MPD officers were assigned to our sector along with the Special Operation Division (SOD). The SOD officer's were specially trained for riot and crowd control and they meant business when they told you to do something. I was assigned to the base of the Lauinger Library steps at 37th Street as there were no barriers at that location. Three SOD officers were there with me and there were a few protestors trying to taunt us into some sort of action. One in particular kept placing his foot over the picket line to get some reaction, but, I kept ignoring it until I'd had enough of his nutty taunting. I sidled my way toward him and as I got near enough I pretended I wasn't looking and just as he placed his foot where it shouldn't have been I stomped down on it with my heel on his toes. Wow! He let out a yell you could have heard all the way in Tehran and the SOD guy's were just laughing their heads off. One of them jokingly told me that if I ever left my job I could work with them any day. On the actual day of the visit of the Shah and his wife I was reassigned to help his security staff bring them on campus without incident, so, I suggested the best route to the campus where there would little, if any, resistance. The motorcade traveled along M Street to Canal Road to the rear parking lot entrance and then proceeded through the parking lot and up the New South roadway to the Healy Building where the Shah and his wife dismounted their limousine, entered the Healy Building, and was escorted to the President's office. The Shah's bodyguards were heavily armed and never more than three feet away from him at all times. The meeting in the President's office lasted about a half hour then the Shah and his entourage departed Healy Building, got back into their limo's and left the campus. Everyone breathed a big sigh of relief after his departure, but, the protestors were still gathered out on the streets and sidewalks. Over the next three days their strength dwindled down to almost nothing and on the fourth day everything was back to normal and we were back on our regular eight-hour shifts. Strangely enough, even with all the security of his bodyguards, as the Shah was in his own home country during some type of ceremony he was assassinated. Thank God that it didn't happen while he was here.

The students of the graduating senior class select their commencement speaker and one year the voted for Pear Bailey. Guest speakers are always awarded an honorary Doctorate degree and Pearl was no exception and as she was ending her speech she made the comment "...now that I have this honorary degree, I guess I'm going to have to earn a real degree." And she did! The following semester she enrolled as a freshman with Georgetown University and attended all her classes as any other student did. Pearl refused getting any slack from her professors and her instructors because of her celebrity status and all the other students adored her. She fit right in with the others and ate the same food in the cafeteria as they did. Whenever she would see any of our officers she would always make it a point to say hello and chat with them for a minute or two. I knew her husband Louie Belson from back home in Illinois. His parents owned a music store in Moline, Illinois. The dividing line between Rock Island and Moline is 52nd Street. Once you cross that street you're in another town. My cousins lived in Moline so I spent quite a bit time there and Louie happened to be one of the guy's that hung around with us. I would see Louie pretty often on campus and we would chew the fat once in a while about old times back home.

We had a student whom I'll call Vince Singer whose home is in Margate, New Jersey. Vince was a severe pain in the neck and at least once a month his name came across my desk in a report for one dumb thing or another...he was constantly on the verge of doing something stupid to be locked up for. One time he tied the hands of a female student to a door handle in Harbin Hall and she had been tied there for almost an hour before someone saw her and contacted campus police. The girl told us who had tied her to the door and I had an officer go to Vince's room and tell him to report to my office as soon as his legs could get him here. Five minutes later Vince was in my office and I went up one side of him and down the other side telling him what kind of trouble he could have caused and all the different laws he broke. This was not the first time Vince had been in my office for some idiotic act he did and he knew without a doubt that I was fired up. I almost placed him under arrest, but thought different of it and decided to take the matter to the Student Adjudication Board because all he would have gotten downtown would be a slap on the wrist as a first time offender. After about twenty minutes of my haranguing Vince I told him he was free to go, but one more stupid incident from him and he'll be spending the night in the Central Cell Block. Vince went before the adjudication and I presented my case as strongly as I could and it resulted in him being suspended from school for the remainder of the semester. One night while Vince was back home in New Jersey he was hitch hiking from Ocean City back to Margate. The driver of a Toyota pick up truck stopped and gave him a ride and somehow the conversation came up about Georgetown University. Vince told the driver about his suspension and about the rotten SOB that caused it. The driver asked who the SOB was and Vince said "...their Chief Investigator, a guy named Sergeant Christian, the bastard." Upon hearing that the driver slammed on his brakes and told Vince to "get the hell out of my truck ". Vince got out and had another twelve miles to go to get back home and the driver sped away leaving Vince alone on a dark and rarely traveled road. The driver of the truck just happened to be George Mauro, my nephew who held me in the highest regard as his uncle. Don't tell me there's no God! When George told me about this incident I laughed for at least a half hour and even to this day when I recall it I still get a smile on my face.

There was a middle aged woman that gave the appearances of being homeless and was always hanging around the perimeter of the campus and whenever there was some type of function where food was being offered she was right there getting her share and filling her pockets. Many times she would sneak into the lower level of Lauinger Library and get into the ladies room and cleaned herself and took care of business. Our officer's responded to the numerous calls we received about her and every time they would escort her off campus with a warning not to return. Talking to her was like spitting into the wind as she made it a point to totally ignore their warnings. Eventually I became involved with her encroachments and gave her the same warnings and made it known to her emphatically that I was extremely serious and would arrest her the next time that she came on university property. As usual with her my warnings fell on deaf ears and two days later as a function was underway in the East Campus quad she just meandered in and was filling her paper plate with food when I approached her, placed her under arrest, put the handcuffs on her, and took her to the O'Gara Building. While in our building I had a female officer perform a "pat down" cursory search of her person and as we searched her purse for identification I couldn't believe what we found. There were three U. S. Government checks totaling more than $4,000 made payable to Mrs. Diane Archer. We were also able to prove that our "homeless lady" was Diane Archer. When I asked her why was she scrounging food when she had enough money to but a hundred sirloin steaks, she merely said "...I really didn't need the money." We allowed her a phone call and she was able to call her son, Gregory, who appeared at our offices in about a half hour. Gregory was only fourteen years old, but I asked him why his mother was living in this manner? Gregory told me that his parents had separated and he was alternating his living between the two parents. At that time he was living with his father who was a professor at George Washington University but didn't provide any financial assistance to his mother. Gregory also explained that the government checks were from Social Security and tax refunds. Considering the circumstances and there being no real harm done I had Mrs. Archer sign a Release for Libel Form and escorted her and Gregory off the campus. I reiterated my warning of Unlawful Entry and made certain that Gregory knew what a violation thereof could entail. I was assured by Gregory that his mother would not come back. Well, at least they kept their promise for about a month, because, as the students were celebrating Senior Week with parties all over the place, beer flowing like the Potomac River and lots of free food, who should appear? None other than Mrs. Archer and her son Gregory. I spotted them as they were getting in a food line and pulled them to the side and asked what they were doing here again after being warned what would happen should they return? Well, this time they thought they pulled a real fast one as they had registered Gregory for summer classes so he could have a Georgetown University ID card giving him permission to be on campus. I advised them that summer classes hadn't started yet and that his ID card was invalid except for attending classes. It did not authorize him and his mother to participate in other university functions, so, they were told that they would have to leave the campus until summer classes started. It got to the point where these two people were a constant thorn in the side. Either they were totally incorrigible and had no respect for authority or they were just plain stupid and didn't care what happened. And then there is the possibility that they just wanted to make my life as miserable as could be. In either case I had our officers keep a tight watch on their activities and report to me if there was any misconduct on their part. In the mean time I did some checking around and discovered that Gregory had not attended any of his classes, so I spoke with the registrar and it was determined that Gregory would be dropped from the rolls and part of his tuition would be refunded. A letter was mailed to Gregory at the address he provided on his registration form, but it was returned with the notation "NO SUCH ADDRESS". In view of this it was necessary to advise him in person as to the action being taken against him for non attendance. There was a reception scheduled for the following day in the Hall of Nations and there was a strong possibility that

Gregory and his mother would be there...they hadn't missed one yet even though they were not invited. A half hour after the reception got underway I and Jim McNally eased our way into the Hall of Nations via the side entrance and just as sure as clock work there was Gregory and mama. We approached them and escorted them outside the building where I advised Gregory that he was no longer a registered student at this university and demanded his university ID card. He surrendered his ID card and both he and his mother were again escorted off campus and in no uncertain terms told that the games were over and there would be no more breaks given and the next time would be lock up time. I might as well have been talking to the wall, because one week later Mrs. Archer was seen in the ladies room of Lauinger Library. I responded to that area and waited for her to exit and as she did I placed her under arrest, cuffed her, and called for a transport to the O'Gara Building where she was again searched by a female officer. At the time of her arrest she also had about ten or twelve loaves of French bread in her possession. The bread was so hard you could drive a nail in with it, but she insisted on keeping them. When the MPD transport unit arrived to take her to Second District they refused to allow the bread in their cruiser because a couple of the loaves were crawling with bugs. The following day I had to appear at the Superior Court to paper the case and once that was done I washed my hands of any further contact with any of the Archers. The only other contact I would have to have with them when would be when I had to appear in Superior Court for their appearance before a judge. I must admit, I think that was about the worst summer I ever had in my sixteen years at Georgetown.

Apartheid means "Separateness" in the Afrikaans language of South Africa. At Georgetown it meant protest and protest meant demonstrations. As I had mentioned earlier students seemed to want to protest about almost anything. Granted, some of their protests had merit while other protests seemed to be something to do in your spare time if you didn't have anything better to do. The protest against Apartheid was a legitimate one that did have merit, but the demonstrations had to be contained and controlled and in good taste. The first demonstration attempt was to stage a sit in at the doors to the office of the University President, Father Timothy Healy. Naturally, this went over like a lead balloon and we "encouraged" the demonstrators to pick another site for their protest. They decided that the front steps of Healy Building would be a terrific location so they began their squatting there. That only lasted for two hours before we again had to "encourage" them to find a different location, so they moved their activities to the big lawn area in front of the White-Gravenor Building where the Admissions Office and Student Loan Office is situated. It wasn't long before they had edged their way onto the plaza area of White-Gravenor and was impeding foot traffic into and out of the building. Officers were dispatched to that location to insure that all entrances and exits were kept clear and business could continue uninterrupted. At the beginning there wasn't really a whole lot of concern placed on the demonstrations as they were peaceful and controlled and it was believed that after a couple of days they would think they'd made their point and call it quits. Their main complaint with the university was that they wanted Georgetown to divest all its interests in South Africa and any other country that is supportive of the Afrikaaner's policy on Apartheid. Well, as it turned out a couple of days passed and they were still sitting out on the lawn and even when the rains came we thought for sure they would give it up, but they hung right in there. The situation also escalated to the point where it took more than just a couple of officer's to keep the entrances clear we also had to insure that the demonstrators did not enter the buildings to use the restrooms. They countered that by renting port-a-potties, but, according to the zoning laws of the District of Columbia these were not authorized for use in a situation or location such as this. In view of the inclement weather they also tried to erect some makeshift shanties which we had to take down and remove. After about a week of these cat and mouse games the administration decided that enough was enough. The demonstrators had their say and it was time now for them to vacate the area and go on about their business of getting an education. The protestors disagreed with this decision and even called on Reverend Jesse Jackson for help. While going into the third week of these demonstrations Jesse Jackson appeared on campus to meet with the administration. I was assigned the duty of accompanying Mr. Jackson wherever he went to insure his safety and escort him to the Presidents office. I have no idea what may have transpired in this meeting, but when Jesse Jackson left the Presidents office he didn't seem too pleased and I didn't see any smile on his face. We went where the demonstrators were sitting and Jesse gave a brief speech and then left the campus. Whatever the demonstrators apparently wanted to happen didn't materialize and the administration decided to take whatever action was necessary to put an end to this situation. Consequently, Mr. Lamb met with the Commander of the Second District and laid out our plan of action and requested their assistance in the form of transport vehicles and possibly some manpower. I was told to come to work the next day dressed in casual clothing rather than a suit and tie, so I came to work in my Levi's, sneakers and pull over shirt. At 8:30am Mr. Lamb, Pete Pervi, Ron Arbogast, my other investigators, and I proceeded to the White-Gravenor lawn. All available officers were also dispatched to that area. Shortly after our arrival five MPD "paddy wagons" showed up on the road way adjacent to the White-Gravenor building. Mr. Lamb, with the help of a bullhorn advised the demonstrators that they were in violation of certain District of Columbia laws and he gave them fifteen minutes to gather their belongings and vacate the area or they would be placed under arrest. There wasn't too much positive response to this announcement, so, Mr. Lamb again repeated what he had said, and about ten or twelve people decided they didn't want any jail time so they grabbed their stuff and left the area. Ten minutes went by and Mr. Lamb made the announcement one more time adding that this was the last warning and in five minutes arrests would be made. Sure enough, no one took any heed to the warning so we started placing the disposable type handcuffs on the demonstrators, but they refused to stand up and had to be carried to the waiting paddy wagons, then they had to be hefted inside to back and still refused to get up or sit on the benches inside, so, we just stacked them on top of each other like cord wood and let them figure it out. The MPD officers were most helpful with this process as they were big guys and they just grabbed the demonstrators by the back of their waists and lift them up like a sack of potatoes and carried them to the paddy wagons. As you might expect all the media was there in all their glory filming everything, so, we had to be extra careful not to use any undue force. It seemed like everyone on campus was at the scene watching the proceedings. It took us about one and a half hours to get them all in transport vehicles and headed to the Central Cell Block. Lt. Sarnie had given the supervisor of the cell block a heads up about all these new arrivals they would be getting and upon their arrival there wasn't any playing around by the jail personnel. If the subjects refused to stand up or walk, as they had when being arrested, they were dragged by the neck of their shirt or blouse (whichever the case may be) and just dumped on the floor at the admissions desk. A special area was set aside for our little angels to separate them from the more criminal elements. Charlie Adkins, Jim McNally, and I went to the AUSA office of the Superior Court to do the papering of all thirty-five people. I was very grateful that Charlie and Jim knew the procedures for papering as it helped out an awful lot and of course we got a certain amount of jibing from the AUSA's who were assigned to paper our cases. By the time we finished with the papering and returned to the O'Gara Building it was close to midnight, so, I told Charlie and Jim that they could come in late the next day and thanked them for a job well done.

There had been several other demonstrations staged by the students, but none quite as time and manpower consuming as the Apartheid demonstrations. One case in particular was when the Federal Communications Commission (FCC) ordered the shut down of the campus radio station WGTB. I don't know why so many people want to try to get away as much vulgarity in public as possible before someone puts their foot down and says "that's enough, knock it off!". That is what happened to WGTB. The station manager had been warned on several occasions to clean up their airways or they would have to face the consequences, but these warnings went unheeded and sure enough the station was ordered to cease all broadcasting. Our department was notified and directed to take the necessary action to secure the station and its entire inventory. Pete Pervi and I were assigned to secure the doors of the station and keep everyone out. The broadcast stations were located in the basement of the Copley Building and the transmitter was located about fifteen miles away on a hill top in Maryland. Needless to say, hundreds of listeners, both students and off campus residents didn't hesitate one minute to get their little protest signs made up and plans made for protesting this action. Pete and I got some pretty hard looks from some of the students as they passed the station doors and we also were the recipients of a few choice words and names. In this line of work you have a fairly tough skin and just let those little barbs roll off and I did pride myself on my self control...at least for the first couple of days. On the third day of our lock-out assignment a group of students were passing by when one of them thought he'd be a wise guy and called over his shoulder "...hey pigs, eat s**t!". Well, that was the straw that broke the camels back. I ran after the group and caught up with them and singled out the big mouth and told the others to go about their business or they'd be in deep trouble too. I took the student into one of the vacant rooms and told him to repeat what he had just said, but, he refused. I lit into him verbally like a Marine Corps drill instructor and came down on him like a ton of bricks. After about ten minutes of a very stern lecture on the proper manner of addressing a police officer the student was shaking for fear of what might happen next and was red faced from embarrassment. When we left the room we proceeded to where Lt. Pervi was standing and the student apologized for his actions and swore that it wouldn't happen again. Apparently, word of this little confrontation must have spread like wild fire, because ever since then when the students passed by our location there was never a derogatory sound. As a matter of fact there were a few "Good morning" or "Good afternoon" salutations offered to us accompanied with a smile or two. And, I was able to resume my self control and composure. It seemed like ages before we could get approval to place our padlocks on the doors and post the appropriate "KEEP OUT" signs on the doors. Both the campus newspapers made a big deal about this station being closed and played it out as long as they could, but eventually everything calmed down and business went on as usual. Several months later the station was allowed to reopen under new management and with the strict stipulation that vulgarity would not be tolerated. Prior to this opening the new station manager came to our department to introduce himself and ask for our assistance as he had made things perfectly clear at a meeting he'd had with the station staff regarding the daily operation of the station and the content of the material that would be broadcast. A lot of these rules didn't sit well with some of the harder core DJ's and they made that fact known to the manager who in turn told them they could find another radio station to work at. We assured the manager of our total support and fortunately the dissidents either accepted the way things were going to be or moved on without incident.

One spring morning after arriving in my office I received a phone call about a possible missing female student. Nancy McDermott's roommate stated that Nancy had not been in her residence hall room nor seen by anyone on campus for two days. I went to the complainant's room and interviewed her and obtained as much information as possible as to Nancy's friends both on and off campus, her habits, her likes and dislikes, and her temperament. A complete search of the campus was conducted with negative findings of her, but her purse was found, intact, in parking lot A which indicated that there may have some foul play involved. I interviewed her roommate a second time to pick her brain for any information she might have concerning Nancy's personal life and if she had any boyfriends she might have had a fight with. Nothing! I contacted the Missing Persons Bureau of the MPD and two detectives responded and were given all the information we had gathered. At this point it became apparent that her parents had to be contacted to determine if she might have gone home unexpectedly, however, her parents had not seen Nancy since her last visit home. Inasmuch as her purse was found the way it was in the parking lot this case was classified as a "Missing Person – Critical". Posters were made up with Nancy's picture and distributed throughout the DC area in addition to the newspapers and the TV stations. MPD also had them transmitted to various other law enforcement agencies in other states. Jeff Horton and I went to her room and sifted through all her personal belongings in hopes of finding some sort of inkling into where she might be. A reporter from one of the TV stations interviewed me concerning the case and kept the story alive with Nancy's picture being shown dozens of time a day. Three days passed and no clue as to her whereabouts when I received a call from a lady at the YWCA (Young Women Christian Association) in Philadelphia, Pennsylvania who stated that there is a girl staying there that looks an awful lot like Nancy. I got all the necessary information and presented it to Mr. Lamb who gave authorization for Jeff and me to go to Philadelphia the next day to make contact and check out the possibility. Upon our arrival in Philadelphia at about 10:00am we reported to the nearest Police Station and identified ourselves and explained our reason for being there. The Philadelphia Police were extremely helpful and offered their assistance as needed. With much anticipation we proceeded to the YWCA and spoke to the lady who had made the call. She informed us that the girl she had told us about had gone out and would return in a couple of hours. Jeff and I decided to have something to eat and then went back to the YWCA where the girl was sitting in the office waiting for us. All my hopes went out the window when I saw that it wasn't Nancy, but there was a very strong resemblance, almost enough that they could be sisters. It was a long shot that didn't pay off, but it had to be done and it was a long dreary ride back to DC. After all possible leads had been followed up and acted upon with negative results I had no choice but to place the case in the "SUSPENDED FILE" awaiting any further leads. In view of this action Jeff and I had to go to Nancy's room and inventory every item that belonged to her and put it all in bags and place it in storage until her parents could come and collect it. It's unbelievable how much stuff students bring with them when they attend college. Two months later I received a call from the Police Department of New London, Connecticut asking about our missing person Nancy. I answered all their questions and provided them with all the information I had available and the detective I spoke to advised me that they had our missing girl. One of their officer's had observed a young girl on a street corner selling newspapers and checked the photo on our flyer and took Nancy into protective custody. I was elated and let out a yell of relief that could be heard all through the department. I felt as though a load of bricks had just been taken off my shoulders. I immediately contacted the MPD detectives and gave them the good news and they too let out a yell of relief. I had also contacted the parents of Nancy, but they informed me they had already been in touch with their daughter and were crying tears of joy. Nancy never did offer any explanation as to her disappearance, however shortly after her return her parents withdrew her from Georgetown and has not been seen nor heard from since. There was some speculation amongst her friends that she had been enrolled in a less academic demanding school, but that is only speculation.

There was another situation where a male sophomore student, Edward Sims was reported missing by his friend, Jeffery Holland. Jeffery stated that he and Edward had been doing some bar hopping on Wisconsin Avenue two nights previously and when they were to meet the following day Edward never showed up. Jeffery just wrote it off as Edward forgetting about the meeting, but after not seeing Edward for two full days he got worried and decided to contact our department. I went through the formalities and the procedures for a missing person and contacted the various hospitals and police departments with negative results. I contacted the Missing Person Section of MPD and gave them all the details and advised them as to the action we had taken and what our future plans were. Jeff Horton and I went to Edward's room to search for any clues as to his whereabouts and the only thing we discovered was a written notation of a United Airline reservation and a flight number and arrival date at Reagan National Airport. I contacted United Airline and explained to them what the situation was and they checked their manifests, but there wasn't anyone listed under the name of Edward Sims. In the event that Edward had used a different name to book a flight that evening Jeff Holland and I proceeded to Reagan Airport to await the arrival of the flight indicated in Edward's note. We watched all the people who had deplaned from that flight, but, there was no sign of Edward. I even approached the flight attendants and showed them Edward's picture, but they didn't recognize him as a passenger on their flight. We returned to the campus and I notified Mr. Lamb of our findings and he in turn advised that he would contact the Dean of Students to notify the parents. The following day I received a call from Mrs. Sims from Florida stating that she and her daughter were on their way to DC and would it be possible to have someone meet them at the airport. I checked with Mr. Lamb for authorization and advised them that I would meet them. That afternoon I met with Mrs. Sims and her daughter Lillian and took them to the hotel where they had reservations. I explained to them what actions we had taken and asked some more pertinent questions as to Edward's likes and dislikes. He liked skiing, but this was summer, so that was no help. He also liked horse back riding, and going to the beach, particularly the ocean. With this information a LOF (Look Out For) was sent to the various police departments along the Atlantic coastline. The situation got to the point where Channel 4 News got involved and came to the campus to interview the Dean of Student Affairs and me and displayed pictures of Edward every half hour asking for information about him. My office was overflowing with phone calls from genuinely concerned citizens to the fringe element that just wants to get their name in a newspaper. Regardless, we followed-up on every phone call with negative results. I and my investigators were working this case around the clock, 24 hours a day pursuing every possible lead no matter how minute it may have seemed. I contacted my friends in the FBI to see if they could lend any assistance or offer any suggestions. They told me that I had covered all the bases and all I could do now was wait to see what transpires. Weeks had passed with no sign of Edward and the case was suspended pending further information or leads. Unfortunately, at the time of my retirement from Georgetown University this case still remained in the unsolved file and as this is being written, to the best of my knowledge, Edward never did return and no one knows whatever happened to that young man. Of course there is the possibility that he returned to his home and his parents just neglected to contact us and let us know, but knowing his parents as I had gotten to know them I doubt that this is the case, however, the possibility of it can't be dismissed.

During the early 1980's there was a situation involving long distance calls being made and being charged to Burt Reynolds telephone. Several of our students were involved and one day I received this phone call from Ms. Annabelle Burns of the C & P Telephone Company. She advised me of the situation and requested my assistance with the interrogation of the involved students. We set a particular date aside to conduct these interrogations and each student was contacted by me and directed to be at my office on that date at 9:00am. It took about three hours to conduct all these interviews and as you can imagine there was quite a bit of complaining on the part of the students about their having to miss their classes (actually, they were all grateful that they didn't have to go to class, but, they had to have something to gripe about). Annabelle called me two days later and advised that she had all the evidence she needed to proceed with prosecution of all these students, however, if we could work out a deal with the students they could be spared a criminal record and a trial. Again, I contacted all the students and advised them that they were facing some serious charges and they were directed to be at my office the following day at 10:00am. Upon their arrival and due to the amount of people we all went into the roll call room where Annabelle explained to them in detail the ramifications of their actions and the possible penalties involved. She also suggested a solution to the problem which was for each student to make full restitution for damages they had incurred. One student had made long distance calls totaling $1,600.00. The rest of them also had made calls of substantial amounts, but not quite that high. In addition they were required to sign a waiver and a Contract of Agreement to the fact that should restitution not be made they would be prosecuted for Theft of Services and Communication Fraud. All the students agreed to Annabelle's plan and she gave them sufficient time to make settlement of their charges. At this point I informed them all that they would also have to appear before the Student Adjudication Board. Annabelle told me that within two weeks she had received all the payments and the case was closed. The Student

Adjudication Board imposed some severe sanctions just short of suspension from school. I felt very certain that they all got the message that "if you do the crime you do the time". Ever since that incident whenever I needed any assistance relating to the telephone company all I had to do was give Annabelle a call. Over the years there had been several occasions for her assistance and we became quite close friends and I couldn't help but admire the spunk and "go get 'em" attitude for a lady up in her years like Annabelle was.

As I had mentioned earlier our responsibilities also extended to the Law Center where Assistant Director Robert T. Robinson was in charge. Robbie and I got along very well and he always appreciated my assistance when they had a problem. I was also on very good terms with the Dean of the Law School, Daniel J. McCarthy who also appreciated the discreet manner in which I conducted my investigations. The Law Center is located downtown not too far from the Superior Court and District Court buildings and it was convenient when I had to appear in court as I could park at the Law Center and have Robbie or one of his officer's give me a ride to the court house. Some guy's hated to have to appear in court as it cut into their off duty time, but they still got paid overtime for it, so I couldn't understand what their complaint was. I rather enjoyed being there as it did give me a chance to get away from the office for a while and see some of my friends from other jurisdictions. There was one time in particular when I was in court for a case I had and as I was waiting for the AUSA to come to the court room I saw this rather tall black man walking (well, more like strutting) down the hallway and from the looks of his attire I would swear that he was a pimp. He was dressed in a pink (yes, pink) suit and was wearing trousers tucked inside the high top boots that laced up the front almost to the knee. He had on an open neck collar shirt and wore almost as much gold around his neck as Mr. T. (from the A-Team TV series). I had to bite my tongue to keep from laughing out loud and after he entered the court room I asked one of the detectives if he knew who that person was. I couldn't believe it when he told me it was Harry T. Alexander. Harry was one of the worst judges that ever sat on a judicial bench. Ninety nine out of one hundred cases he would rule in favor of the defendant. As a matter of fact during one trial he called one of the testifying detectives a liar right in open court. Everyone in the court room heard him as soon as the detective left the witness stand he went directly to MPD Headquarters (which was the next building to the court house) and filed an official complaint against the judge. This was the primary instrument in addition to hundreds of other complaints filed by other law enforcement officer's that opened the door for Harry's removal from the bench. And every law enforcement officer in the District of Columbia breathed a heavy sigh of relief with his removal. To be honest, it was a time for celebration. I was very fortunate that I never had a case heard in Harry's courtroom or the courtroom of Judge Halleck. Judge Halleck was another one of those liberal judges that leaned over backward in favor of the criminal element. To the best of my knowledge Halleck never got removed from the bench but there were all kinds of law enforcement officer's wishing that he would.

Fortunately the Law Center didn't have too many problems, but they did have some that required my attention. Almost all of these situations involved employees in that area. One such case dealt with theft from various offices. There was never anything really expensive being taken, but many of the stolen items had a certain amount of sentimental value attached to them. I met with Robbie and he showed me the various crime scenes and provided me with the time frames when the items were last seen and when they were discovered missing. Based on the information I had available it appeared that surveillance would be called for with the use of the theft detection powder. The contract cleaning personnel didn't report for work until after all the study areas had been closed at midnight, so I met with Robbie at 10:00pm and we placed some recorded money that had been treated in five different offices. In addition to the money we also placed a few watches and a few rings in other offices, and then we went to Robbie's office to wait for the cleaners to do their work. Prior to the cleaners leaving Robbie and I proceeded to the offices where we had placed the treated items and discovered that certain items were missing, mainly the treated money and a couple of the watches and rings. At this point we contacted the supervisor of the cleaning crew to ascertain who had the responsibility of cleaning those particular offices. We then had the supervisor take us to those workers and we escorted them to Robbie's office. While one worker was being interrogated a uniformed officer watched the others to make certain nothing was hidden or disposed of. On the way to Robbie's office one of the female employees was observed putting something in one of the wall ashtrays which was assumed to be some gum. At the beginning of each interview with the suspects I extended my hand with my palm down to shake their hand making it so their palm would be face up where I could see if there were any traces of the theft detection powder. The first two employees were released with no further action, however, the hands of the third one, a female, were so stained with the purple powder it was evident that she had come in contact with the either the money of the jewelry. Naturally she denied everything, but, I noticed a trace of the purple stain near the top of her blouse indicating that she had possibly placed something inside her undergarment that had been treated with the powder. In view of this we had to call for a female officer to come to the scene and the only one we had available was on the main campus, so we had the watch commander drive her to the Law Center and upon her arrival she was briefed about the operation and proceeded to search the suspect in private. No contraband was found on the suspect, but there were a lot of purple stains on her bra, so, I retraced my steps to the wall ashtray and there I found three twenty dollar bills all wadded up into a small ball. With the use of surgical gloves these same bills were straightened out and the serial numbers were checked against those that had been recorded earlier. As expected, they all matched and the purple stain was very evident. The suspect was escorted to where her purse was and directed to empty her purse which produced two of the treated rings and three of the treated watches. At this point the suspect was read her Miranda Warning and placed under arrest. The other employees were cleared of any wrong doing and were released. The suspect was transported by a female MPD Officer to the First District for booking and then to the Central Cell Block.

About two months after this incident various little anti-Semitic signs started appearing at numerous locations around the law center. Some were posted on bulleting boards, some were taped to the elevator interior, and many were placed inside text books in the library. No one had a clue as to who was responsible for these little missives of bigotry, but again I had another meeting with Robbie and Dean McCarthy. To some people this may seem a harmless prank or someone's idea to blow off some steam or to vent their feelings about a certain ethnic group. Whatever the reason was immaterial as it would not be tolerated at the law center. I even thought that it was childish and immature for a law student to engage is this sort of activity. Inasmuch as this would require the use of surveillance cameras and the fact that we only had two available created somewhat of a problem. Additionally, due to the interior design of the building determining where to place these cameras was another problem. Within two days I had the cameras mounted and in operation. Fortunately, many of these messages were hand written, so I did have some physical evidence to work with. The only thing was that there were about 2,000 law students and matching the hand writing of one person out that many people would be a monumental task. After careful examination of the hand writing it was determined that there was only one person involved. It seemed very unlikely that a person of the Jewish faith would write these notes, so I was able to temporarily eliminate all the Jewish students. I assigned Charlie Adkins to assist me in this investigation as he had had prior experience with hand writing analysis. I also assigned Jim McNally to take care of the changing of the film in the cameras and having it developed. I interviewed all the professors at the law center in an attempt to gather what information I could and get what feedback there might be concerning their ideas or suggestions as to who might be the responsible person for the messages. This case was eating up a lot of my time and I had to leave what cases there were at the main campus to the other two investigators of my office. All the bulletin boards were checked daily for new messages and during the third week into the case Jim McNally advised me that we had some good pictures with the date and time of a suspect posting messages on a particular bulleting board. These were the same messages that I had removed the previous day. With this information we went to Dean McCarthy's office and asked him if he could identify the person in the film.

The Dean identified the suspect as James Whitmore, a freshman student. With this information I proceeded to the Registrar's Office and reviewed Mr. Whitmore's records and obtained samples of his signature and other writings. I had friends that worked in the Questionable Documents Section of MPD, so I made my phone call and explained to them what I was working on and they told to bring my material over to them and they would run an analysis on the documents. Three days later I got a call from them telling me they had made a positive match on several of the documents and provided me with an affidavit as to their findings along with the sample documents. I had Jim remove the cameras and told him and Charlie to return to the main campus and continue their normal duties. I produced all the evidence I had along with my written report in chronological order to Dean McCarthy. Mr. Whitmore was summoned to the Dean's office where he was confronted with the evidence and in the presence of Robbie and me the Dean demanded an explanation for his actions. All of a sudden all hell broke loose as Whitmore had flipped his cool and started throwing things around the office, and turning over chairs and tables before Robbie and I could subdue him and get him in handcuffs. At this point Whitmore was placed under arrest for Destruction of Property, Disorderly Conduct, and Simple Assault (I caught a fist in the face during the struggle with him). It turned out that Whitmore was heavy into the white supremacy movement and upon graduating from law school he was going to be defense council (pro bono) for anyone arrested or on trial for race related crimes. Needless to say, Mr. Whitmore never did get his law degree and as a matter of fact after his case came to trial (without a jury) the Judge gave him three years to think things over in the prison at Lorton, Virginia. I must admit that I did feel rather gratified knowing Whitmore was going to do some time because I thought his actions, especially for a law student, was deplorable.

Doctor Isaac Kaplan of the Dental Clinic called me one morning and asked if I could come by his office to discuss a rather important and delicate matter. Prior to lunch I made some time available and met with the doctor who advised me that he was having a problem with money disappearing from accounts payable. He didn't want to suspect the person responsible for handling that money, but the money started missing only since she had started working there. I got all the information I could concerning the suspect, Naomi Cummings and ran a criminal check on her through NCIC. The check came back negative for any criminal record, so we went to the theft detection powder again. Dr. Kaplan provided us with $150.00 cash which we recorded the serial numbers of and treated with theft detection powder. We typed up an envelope addressed to the Dental Clinic Accounts Payable. We also typed up a phony letter explaining this money to be credited to a fictitious account. We inserted the money and the letter in the envelope and then went to the post office on campus and had it postmarked. We then proceeded to the area near the dental clinic to wait for the mail delivery person to arrive. Upon the arrival of the mail person we gave him the letter and instructed him to be sure to give it personally to the suspect. At the same time I had Sylvester Julian inside the dental clinic where he could see everything that took place and also keep track of the baited letter. The accountant opened the letter and searched the files but couldn't find an account for the person who signed the letter (me). Shortly before quitting time I entered the dental clinic complaining about a tooth ache and demanded to see Doctor Kaplan to have it taken care of. The way I was carrying on I thought Sylvester was going to bust out laughing, but he gave me the signal that the suspect had placed the envelope in her purse so I gave him the signal to wait outside for her to exit the building. I got into Dr, Kaplan's office and advised him what was happening and then I joined up with Sylvester outside just before the suspect left the building. As she approached us we identified ourselves and showed her our badges and we all returned inside the dental clinic. Once inside the building we directed the suspect to empty her purse. She refused to comply, so I placed her under arrest and pursuant to an arrest I searched her purse for any weapons and during this search I discovered an envelope addressed to the dental clinic. At this point I read the suspect her Miranda Warning and called our dispatcher to have MPD send a transport unit to the dental clinic. While waiting for the transport unit I opened the envelope and with surgical gloves that I had gotten from Doctor Kaplan I removed the money which was still intact. The serial numbers matched the ones on the list I had made and these items were placed in an evidence envelope. Prior to the arrival of the transport unit the suspect's husband appeared in his car at the curb in front of the dental clinic and I went out to let him know that his wife had been arrested and was being charged with Felony Larceny after Trust. It goes without saying that he flew off the handle and started ranting and raving and carrying on until I was able to get him to settle down and listen to what I had to tell him. I suggested that he get a good attorney for his wife and told him where he should go to make bail for her. I also gave him a few minutes with her before she was transported away and I advised her that the stain on her hands would fade away in a few days. He was grateful for that time with his wife but, I could see it in his eyes that he didn't like me one iota. Not even a little bit.

The Animal Vivarium comes under the Medical Center as it houses the poor animals that are used for medical experiments. I am strongly against the use of animals for this sort of activity, but I had my job to do as much as I disliked this part of it.   A   well known animal rights group decided to stage a protest against the use of these animals for experimentation and in doing so they established a picket line of sorts with their various pro animal rights signs. I was sympathetic to their cause but, as I said I had a job that had to be done and had to put all personal feelings to one side. It became known that an attempt was going to be made to penetrate the vivarium and release all the animals. This would be very noble gesture; however, some of these animals had already been subjected to and injected with various types of diseases and releasing them to their freedom could cause the spread of critical diseases. In view of this I and two of my investigators changed into casual clothes and proceeded to the vivarium where we placed ourselves in strategic locations where we could observe all entrances and exits of the vivarium. After about an hour three people, unknown to us, approached one of the doors to the building and attempted to gain entry. I approached the individuals and identified myself and asked if there were something I could help them with to which they replied that they wanted to go inside the vivarium. I requested some form of identification from them and asked their reason to go inside. During this exchange Jim McNally and Charlie Adkins had come to my location and recorded the identification offered by these people. Once their identity had been established I issued them all a warning about their being on private property and they were subject to arrest, however they were merely being warned at this time and then we escorted them back to public property, to wit, the sidewalk in front of the Medical Center. Slowly the amount of protestors got larger and larger causing the use of additional uniformed officer's to respond to the scene. It should be noted that this demonstration was rather peaceful with the exception of the loud chanting on their part. This chanting caused a lot of the citizens in the area to call MPD and lodge complaints of disorderly conduct. Two patrol cars responded from Second District and I met with the officer in charge and filled him in on the situation and told him that we had everything under control but, he thought it would be a good idea for them to stand by to see what might transpire. After about an hour into this demonstration a TV crew appeared but, once they saw who the demonstrators were they got back into their van and left the scene. This action took the wind out of their sails and seeing that they were not going to get any TV coverage they decided to disperse and end the protest. It took a while for everything to get back to normal and inasmuch as I had suspicions that something else was going to happen at the vivarium Charlie and I set up a surveillance of the area. After a couple of hours and just as it was starting to get dark and I was just about to end the surveillance I saw the same three people we had made contact with previously sneaking around near one of the doors to the vivarium. Charlie and I watched them for about fifteen minutes and when one of them forced open a window. We came down on them and placed them under arrest for Unlawful Entry, Destruction of Property, and attempted Breaking and Entering. All three were placed in handcuffs, Mirandized, and taken to the O'Gara Building where we obtained written statements from all three and then were surrendered to the MPD transport units that responded to our call. While I was at Second District booking these suspects it became apparent that they wanted some media coverage (I guess for publicity for their cause) and they used their one allowed phone call to call one of the TV stations rather than an attorney. No one from the media ever showed up at Second District and the three were then transferred to the Central Cell Block. As I had mentioned earlier, I am sympathetic to their cause but, there are right ways and wrong ways to do things and breaking into buildings is not the right thing to do regardless of how noble your notions may be. The following day at the AUSA office in Superior Court I discussed the situation with the papering AUSA and he agreed to prosecute the case. The trial was before a judge (without a jury) and all three were found guilty of the charges against them and each one received a sentence of full restitution for damages, $250.00 fine, two years probation and no jail time. In addition, the judge issued a restraining order for the entire group barring them from Georgetown University and its property for ten years. To really put the icing on the cake they never did make the papers or any of the TV channels for the publicity they so dearly wanted.

Georgetown University also has satellite offices away from the main campus and we had taken a few reports of thefts from offices at these various locations. Early in the morning on one particular Friday I received a phone call from the manager of one of these departments requesting a security briefing (or seminar if you will) for their personnel. Inasmuch as crime prevention programs was part of my responsibilities I made arrangements to be at their location that afternoon.

At around 2:00pm I met with the supervisor of the department and we proceeded to their conference room where all the employees were assembled. There were about twenty-two employees with the majority being females. The office building they occupied was on Prospect Street in the Georgetown area of the District of Columbia. There were no security officers at any of the entrances so anyone from the street had access. In view of the make up of the personnel present the first thing I did was ask them if they knew where their purses were.

All the ladies looked at each other and I could see a slight look of fear on their faces...the look of a victim of a purse theft. At that point I gave them sufficient time to go to their respective offices and retrieve their purses. Once that matter was out of the way I then asked if they had locked their office doors after getting their purses. Maybe one or two had taken that precaution, but the majority of them hadn't taken the time to do that. I couldn't afford any more delays, so I proceeded with my safety and security presentation. I advised them about calling our department if the observed any suspicious looking persons in their area; I told them how to secure their personal property while at work and gave them advice as to their personal safety. The entire presentation lasted for almost an hour and a half and I covered every possible area I could think of and had a question and answer period afterward. I must have fielded at least fifteen different questions and at the end I got a very rousing applause and an appreciative thank you.

Upon returning to my office I spoke with Mr. Lamb about a plan I had thought of to see if the presentation I had given really had any affect on their work habits as regards to safety and security. He agreed with my plan and encouraged me to follow it through, so, all weekend I didn't shave and on Monday when I left my house for work I was dressed in old street clothes that should have been donated to the trash can two years ago and carried my other work clothes in a garment bag and had them in the trunk of my car. I proceeded to the department where I had given my safety and security presentation the previous Friday. Had I been a thief I could have gotten enough valuables and money that morning to make my mortgage payment. After meandering around their office areas for half an hour without being challenged I then went to the supervisor who, at first glance, didn't recognize me and told him that my visit on Friday had been an exercise me futility. I advised him that there were serious security and safety violations that should be addressed as soon as possible before someone became a theft or rape victim. I asked him to accompany me as I pointed out the various lack of security of personal property (purses, watches, rings and other jewelry) in addition to the potential loss of university property. He had a very red face and I couldn't determine if it was from embarrassment or anger about the lack of security exercised by his employees. After a brief discussion with him I then continued to my office where I shaved, dressed into my working clothes and met with Mr. Lamb and advised him of my findings that morning. It was then that it was decided to make random unannounced visits to various departments and record their safety/security deficiencies and then write a memo to the department head advising him/her of their potential problems. It goes without saying that this program didn't set too well with some of the department heads but, after an explanation and discussion about our reasons for these actions they all agreed that it was a good idea and offered their one hundred percent support. It should be noted that office thefts took a steep decline.

The East Campus complex was the source of many reports ranging from unlawful entry to narcotics dealings. Another area of concern was the fact that the third floor men's room of the Walsh Building had been mentioned in one of the gay oriented newspapers in the District as a delightful meeting place for gays. Consequently, this area required special attention, especially during the evening hours. Having a uniformed officer make frequent patrols of the area did have some affect but, the problem still existed and actually almost got out of control. It was during this time when I would stay after duty hours and cruise the area in my plain clothes. After about two nights of watching the men's room and seeing a couple males enter and stay for a longer than normal time I entered the bathroom and pretended to take care of business and then went to the door and opened and let it close. I stayed inside, motionless and listened. I heard one of them say "I think it's okay now" and then I heard some other noises that were indistinguishable. Very quietly I knelt down on my knees so I could look under the stalls from one end and I saw a set of feet facing the wall of the stall and I saw someone on the other side of the wall in a kneeling position. This was a real no brainer, so, I eased my way to the stall next to where the action was, entered and stood on the toilet seat so I could look into the other stall. Unnoticed I said "having a good time gentlemen?" and both men almost had a cardiac arrest. I broke up their little love tryst and inasmuch as homosexuality is not a crime in the District of Columbia the only other course of action was to charge them with unlawful entry if they weren't Georgetown students. As it turned out neither one of the "lovers" was a student of Georgetown, so I placed them under arrest for unlawful entry and called the dispatcher on the radio for transport to the O'Gara Building. In view of the fact that at that time I only had one set of handcuffs I placed one handcuff on the left wrist on one of them and the other to the right ankle of the other person. If they were entertaining any thoughts of trying to run away it was very doubtful that they would get very far without attracting someone's attention. The next day maintenance personnel had to respond to that restroom to cover up the "glory holes" that had been made by someone with a lot of time on their hands. There were four stalls in that bathroom and three "glory holes" that maintenance had to cover. After a few more nights like that with arrests made a brief notice appeared in the same homosexual oriented newspaper that Walsh Building meetings were bad news and best not to go there.

Because of its proximity to the Georgetown area of the District we were very vulnerable to all sorts of outsiders coming onto the campus. Inasmuch as Georgetown University is a pretty affluent institution thieves were drawn there like ants on candy, I mean why go to a poor area to steal something when you can go to a rich neighborhood and steal better and more expensive things. And it should be noted that students, no matter what school they're at, are extremely careless with their belongings. That's why the thieves prey on college campuses. As I had mentioned earlier though, the students aren't the only careless ones, the employees are too. While on the other hand they do, at times, display a certain amount of vigilance and contact our office when something or someone seems suspicious in nature and we respond to investigate these calls. That accounts for so many arrests made for unlawful entry and burglary II cases. It is a good thing that there's no law against stupidity because if there were the jails would be overflowing and there wouldn't be any room for the real criminals.

There was one incident involving a cross dresser or transvestite who was sashaying down the hall of Healy basement making obscene gestures and comments to everyone he came in contact with. I happened to be in the area at that particular time and responded to the call for a suspicious person in Healy basement. I observed the person in question and approached him and asked for some form of identification. He stated that he didn't have to show me anything and that this was a free country and he could do as he pleased. It was apparent this person was going to give me problems, so I called the dispatcher for a back-up unit. Upon their arrival I tried to get the subject into an area away from the general public, however, he refused to move and started spewing swear words left and right and made all sorts of vulgar comments about me and my mother. I advised him to watch his language, but it was like talking to the wall, so, I advised him that he was under arrest for unlawful entry and disorderly conduct and I instructed him to turn around, face the wall, extend both hands, and lean against the wall. At this point he got very belligerent and refused to comply so I spun him around and placed him up against the wall and proceeded to handcuff him when he started to put up some resistance. To protect my self I placed one foot behind his left knee and applied pressure that caused the knee to bend and forced him to a kneeling position. In doing so his face scraped against the wall which was made of bricks resulting in a few minor scratches. I finally had him handcuffed and took him to the patrol car for transport to the O'Gara Building. As the subject was placed into the transport vehicle of MPD he looked at me and stated "I'm going to go to my house and get my big gun and come back here and shoot you." I guess I was supposed to have been intimidated by that so called threat, but, I just couldn't visualize him having the muscles to hold a gun, so I just shrugged it off. My actions were observed by one of the bleeding heart students who had filed a complaint against me for excessive force. The next day I was called into Mr. Lamb's office where I was advised of the complaint. I explained the situation and the reason for the action I took. My explanation satisfied him and he in turn notified the student that the matter had been taken care of. He additionally advised the student that there were times when excessive force is required and he should just accept that fact.

In all my years at Georgetown I was called in to the boss's office only one other time for excessive force, however this time it was justified also. It all started over a call we had received concerning a suspicious character on Healy lawn wearing some sort of a uniform. It was a beautiful warm spring day and everyone wanted to be outdoors enjoying the weather. That even includes the patients at St. Elizabeth's Mental Hospital in the District. One of their patients had escaped their grounds and ended up on our campus. A couple of days earlier I had read a bulletin sent out from St. Elizabeth's concerning a missing patient and from the description given in that bulletin this person was a perfect match. I contacted St. Elizabeth's Security Office and advised them that we might have their missing patient and requested any additional information on the subject. I was advised that the patient thinks that he is General Douglas MacArthur (of World War II fame) and can be violent at times if he gets really riled. I was also advised that they were sending officer's to our location to take the patient back to St. Elizabeth's. This information was passed on to all the officers in the field and they were directed to just keep the subject under observation. I responded to where the sighting occurred and observed the subject for about ten minutes wishing for the hospital security personnel to hurry and get there as I had never had to deal with any real mental patients like this one. After keeping him under observation for about fifteen minutes he appeared to get a little edgy and gave the appearance that he was going to leave the campus which I wouldn't have had any problem with except for the fact that I had already told the hospital security supervisor at St. Elizabeth's that we would hold him until they arrived to take custody of him. I saw that he was heading toward to main gate, so I ran there to intercept him and try to cajole him to stay on campus. I beat him to the gate and as he approached I came to attention and saluted him and said "Good afternoon, General" and he saluted me back and asked me what outfit I was with. I relied on my military experiences and told him the 25th Infantry Division to which he replied "that's a very good outfit." At this point I made up a long story about some military problems we were having and wanted his advice on how to resolve them.

In doing so I suggested, in an effort to keep his mind occupied, that we have a seat to discuss them. Just as we were about to get into a discussion he saw the St. Elizabeth's security officer's approaching and started to bolt for the main gate. Everything happened so fast he caught me off guard and I chased after him. As we neared the gate he stopped all of a sudden and just stood still. I stopped too and then continued walking toward him. I got to him and told him that he had to go back to the hospital, but he refused and started to get in a nasty mood, so, I told him it was for his own good and the troops there really needed him. He ignored that comment and started to leave again when one of the St. Elizabeth's security officers who were running toward us called to me to keep him from getting away, so, I ran after him and tackled him and put a choke hold on him. While we were struggling on the ground he struck me near the left eye with his elbow and then I used my martial arts training and placed him in a cross choke hold. By this time the St. Elizabeth's security officers arrived at our scene and placed him in handcuffs. I asked them what took them so long to get to where we were and they stated that they were moving as fast as they could and apologized for my getting hit by their patient. This whole incident was observed by at least two dozen people and one of them thought that I was being too rough on the subject and filed a complaint for using too much force. As expected I was called into Mr. Lamb's office again the following day to explain my actions and once he saw the bruise near my eye he told me I'd done a good job and to forget about the complaint. As far as he was concerned it looked like self defense and he said he'd take care of it. That was the end of that complaint. If the "bleeding hearts" only knew half of the situations we run across or get involved in they would be a lot more reluctant to stick their noses in where they're not wanted. Granted, there are times when excessive is used and may get out of hand, but, those are rare exceptions.

There was an incident involving the theft of a sign-in book at one of the residence halls (Harbin Hall) and the suspect was a student whose father was a member of the Board of Trustees and allegedly the richest man in Hong Kong, China. The sign-in book had no intrinsic value to it, but, the content of the book was very important to an ongoing drug dealing investigation. Consequently, the suspected student was called to my office where he was given his Miranda warning and questioned about the disappearance of the sign-in book. He denied any knowledge of the incident and when he was advised that we had an eye witness that saw him take it he immediately asked for an attorney, so, I stopped the interview and let him leave temporarily to get a lawyer. Apparently that evening he called his father in Hong Kong and told him about my questioning him because the very next morning as soon as I walked in the door of the O'Gara Building I was told I had a phone call. I picked up the phone and the caller identified himself as Eric Hotung and proceeded to read me the riot act about his son not being a criminal and how wrong I was by even questioning him and his integrity and I was going to be in real deep trouble because of it. I was barely given a chance to get a word in, and when I could I advised him that it was a standard procedure to question all suspects in a crime. At this point I thought Mr. Hotung was going to blow a gasket the way he was sputtering and yelling on the phone, so, I just listened to him rant and rave. Fortunately, all of our telephone calls are recorded and I made a copy of this call and went directly to the office of the Dean of Student Affairs and played it to Dean John (Jack) DeGioia. I also advised the Dean that I did not appreciate some parent calling me and yelling at me the way this person did regardless of how much juice he had with the university. The Dean saw that I was extremely hot under the collar and stated that he would handle the matter and get back to me. I also informed Mr. Lamb about this incident and at that time I was informed of Mr. Hotungs standing and position with the university. As a father I would more than likely have done the same thing, but I would have checked into the accusations first before doing a lot of ranting and raving and making threats. At any rate the sign-in book was mysteriously returned and we were able to conclude the ongoing investigation with positive results and a few arrests. As I write this it should be noted that Jack DeGioia is now the President of Georgetown University and I recently read that a new building at the Law Center had been donated by Eric Hotung and that he was still a member of the Board of Trustees for Georgetown University. By the way, I still have the tape of that conversation from Hong Kong.

On 7 September 1990 I left work a little early and stopped on the way home to buy a birthday cake as it was my wife's birthday and I had plans of taking her out for dinner. I arrived home and upon entering the house I saw my wife lying sprawled on the kitchen floor with her back resting against a chair that had been tipped over. I called to her and got no response and went to her side an knelt down to feel for a pulse...there wasn't one and there was no sign of any breathing and she felt cool to the touch. The telephone receiver was out of the cradle and the phone was lying on the floor also. I immediately dialed 911 and told the dispatcher that my wife was dead and to send someone right away. I then went outside, lit a cigarette and waited for the police to arrive.

I also called my office and told them of my findings and that I wouldn't be in for work for a while. I then contacted my best friend Kevin McCarthy who came to my house as fast as he could and gave me the support I needed. Kevin even called my sons and I spoke to them and told them what had happened. Shortly after the police arrived and questioned me the Medical Examiner arrived and did what he had to do and then they removed my wife and took her to a funeral parlor that Kevin had suggested. Inasmuch as Kevin had recently had his father interred at Arlington National Cemetery, he made all the arrangements for Mary to be placed there too in the columbarium. I appreciated all that Kevin and his family had done for us as he stayed right with us the whole time making arrangements for this or that. A few days later we had the services for Mary at the Fort Myer Chapel followed by her being placed in a niche of the columbarium.

After the ceremonies were over my sons both suggested that I retire from Georgetown University and move to another area. I agreed and we put our house up for sale and I submitted my papers for retirement. I then found a house in Tappahannock, Virginia and I moved there and waited for the settlement of my house in Arlington. The rest is history.

So, on 1 October 1990 my career ended as Chief Investigator of the Georgetown University Police Department. I'd had sixteen wonderful years doing a job that I really loved doing and meeting some of the greatest people in the world...people that I will never forget until my dying day. All the members of the Georgetown University community, the MPD cops that I'd had the pleasure to work with, all the federal agents that became my friends and cohorts and all the other law enforcement personnel.

I'm certain there were many more stories that I could have included in this book, but, after 15 years the memory gets a little hazy and I feel privileged that I was able to recall all these stories. It really was an exciting period of my life filled with new experiences every single day.